HOW TO REPAIR YOUR MARRIAGE:

Easy Steps to Rekindle the Love and Passion

Nelly V. Venturini

DISCLAIMER

This book is designed to provide accurate information in regard to the subject matter covered, and every effort has been made to ensure that it is correct and complete. The author is not providing professional advice or services to the reader, and this book is not intended as a substitute for the professional services of a psychotherapist, marriage counselor, psychologist, clinical social worker, or other similar professional.

The reader should consult such a professional in matters related to serious marital problems, mental health concerns, and particularly with respect to any of the conditions or situations listed in Part 3: "Special Circumstances" of this publication, which may require professional attention.

There is a list of additional resources in Part 3 of this publication where the reader may find helpful information. The author of this book is not responsible for any of the content, claims, accuracy, or representations of such sources.

All names and details of cases and individuals mentioned in this publication have been changed to protect their privacy.

To my God, who has loved me unconditionally in my life's journey.

To my Mother and Aunt, who loved me deeply and inspired me to become who I am today.

To my wonderful husband, who has been my best friend, has helped me learn the true meaning of love, and has been my greatest cheerleader in writing this first publication.

INDEX

PART 3

FOREWORD

This publication is designed to help you learn basic principles that can help you in the creative journey of building an intimate relationship that is meaningful, loving, and satisfying. I invite you to embrace this process of discovery about yourself, your partner, and the incredible possibilities for your relationship.

Do you recall falling in love with your partner? I bet you do, without having to try too hard. Close your eyes and think back to those early days of your relationship. You may recall that falling in love happened naturally, and being in love was fun and exciting. Everything seemed right between the two of you. As a matter of fact, it felt so right that you wanted it to last forever, which led you to make the decision to marry.

You probably imagined that being with your partner would permanently ensure that the special connection you shared would always be there. You had dreams and desires that you thought would become a reality in your marriage, and all would be well in the universe. In such a blissful state you probably also assumed that the fun, aliveness, and passion would never end, and that you and your partner would have a fairy tale ending to your love story.

I can tell you that you are in great company. The great majority of people can identify with you experience because that is the nature of romantic love. This is how couples begin their relationship journey together, and what they expect in marriage. Romantic love is a very important stage in the development of a committed relationship. It is the beginning of a powerful experience that can transform one's life.

Many couples believe that the romantic love they share will last a lifetime in a natural and easy way. You and your spouse, like most marriage partners, may erroneously believe that keeping your love alive should not take hard work. You probably want it to be easy, and to continue flowing like a natural spring you can drink from without exhausting its source. You may also think that true love happens by sheer desire and by the magic chemistry between you. Indeed, at the beginning it does for most couples, but not so as time goes by.

What you and your partner probably did not realize at the beginning of your relationship is that preserving this loving connection over time would be challenging, and that it would take a lot of work. Maintaining a strong and secure connection in marriage is, without doubt, one of the most important endeavors in life. And it can also be one of the most rewarding, yet challenging ones because it requires consistent commitment and effort over a lifetime.

As a couple both of you need to work hard at creating and maintaining those loving feelings as time evolves. But the majority of couples lack the necessary skills to make their love last, and to make their marriage work.

Chances are that you and your husband have already experienced a myriad of difficult emotions like surprise, disappointment, confusion, or even anger and sadness when you find yourselves lost in the process of watching your marriage deteriorate. Not knowing where to go from there to bring the love and passion back into your marriage may keep you bewildered and disoriented.

But I have good news for you! The skills that you need to keep your marriage alive can be learned. With effort and determination your desire to love and be loved can become a reality as you apply the principles and steps outlined in this book.

STEP 1 – DO I NEED THIS BOOK?

If you are hesitant or ambivalent about reading this book, or even wonder if you need to read it, I invite you to take a few moments so you can honestly answer the following questions:

- Is your marriage "good enough", but not quite what you dreamed of?

- Do you feel emotionally disconnected from your partner?

- Do you feel lonely in your marriage?

- Do you feel hurt, resentful, disappointed, criticized or rejected by your spouse?

- Do you find yourself longing for the love and passion you had in the beginning of your relationship, but don't know what to do to bring them back?

- Do you find that you and your partner argue with increasing frequency, but the issues don't get resolved?

- Do you find yourself tiptoeing around your partner to avoid "rocking the boat" in your relationship?

- Has the emotional connection in your marriage faded to the point where talking, having fun, and being sexually intimate leave you yearning for more?

- Have you noticed that you and your partner tend to get more defensive and overreact when you disagree?

- Do you find yourself reaching out to family members, friends, or co-workers to talk about your partner or your marital problems?

- Do you get the love, attention, and support you

need from these external sources because you don't get that from your partner?

If you answered "yes" to any of the above questions, then this book is for you. It can help you get a fresh start, so be hopeful. In my years of practice as a Marriage Therapist and Couples' Coach, I know that even when only one of the marriage partners learns the necessary skills for creating a healthy marriage, the "power of one" can make a significant difference.

So if you have been tempted to give up on your most important relationship, I urge you not to until you have given this book a try. You won't regret it. The skills you will find in this book are proven methods for improving, and even saving a marriage. I have taught these to many couples and individuals in my years of practice as a Certified Imago Relationship Therapist and Marriage Coach. In my work with couples I have witnessed great outcomes when courageous people exercise their ability to go after what they want in their marriage.

I also know that the skills I teach in this book work because I use them in my own marriage. Much of my training has required me to experience the process of learning and using these skills prior to teaching them to those who seek my assistance. These tools have helped me to become a better wife, a better therapist, even a better person.

Additionally, I have taken a great deal of time and effort

to develop approaches and interventions based on my clinical and personal knowledge, which have proven to be highly effective for other people as well.

The unfortunate truth is that most partners relate to each other in ways that do not allow their relationship to reach its full potential, so they settle for less, sometimes for very little. Many couples live their lives in "quiet desperation" as Henry David Thoreau said once. It is no wonder there are so many unhappy marriages, high divorce rates, and rampant extra-marital affairs.

But if that is where you are today, it is not where you have to stay. I can only surmise that, since you have made the smart and courageous decision to seek information on how to improve your marriage, it's because you want more than what you currently have, and you are willing to go the extra mile. I applaud you for that!

So I have more good news for you. You can DEFINITELY have more than what you've had in your marriage so far. Creating a happy marriage is within your reach. My goal in writing this book is to help you meet your needs and expectations for experiencing love as a creative, meaningful, and fulfilling force in your life and marriage.

To start this process, I challenge you to start viewing yourself and your partner as separate individuals, and your marriage as the sacred interpersonal space that exists between you and your partner. That sacred space is where the "us" takes place. It is distinct from each of you, and it has elements of both of you at the same time. I challenge you now to make a solid commitment to fulfill your personal responsibility for filling this space with the best that you can offer.

As I said before, this book involves learning principles and concepts, as well as doing exercises to put them into practice. This is how you will be able to integrate intellectual knowledge with personal experience, which can make all the difference in the world. Indeed, the difference will be between having an unhappy, average, or mediocre marriage, and enjoying a marriage that is loving, vibrant, passionate, meaningful, lasting, and satisfying.

As you begin this process, I want to encourage you to become curious about what this journey in life will be like for you and your husband. Being curious will open your heart and your mind to new possibilities. It will allow you to get a new perspective from which you can generate positive change. It will also allow you to think differently so that you can start feeling and acting more positively.

Helping people improve or save their marriage has been my passion over the years, and I am very grateful for the opportunity to touch their lives. My goal in writing this book is to assist more people like yourself, and I hope that it helps you in your personal journey. I consider it a privilege to be a part of this transformative process, and I wish you the best.

To your life and marriage,

Nelly

PART 1

CHAPTER 1: THE TRUTH ABOUT LOVE AND MARRIAGE

"There is more hunger for love in this world than for bread." Mother Theresa

I once heard the minister at a wedding say that happiness in marriage has more to do with being the right partner, than expecting your spouse to be the right partner for you. What a concept! I am sure there were many in the audience pondering that statement. In my experience as a couple's therapist and marriage coach, I can attest to the validity of such wisdom because that is truly what marriage is about.

In time you may also come to agree that the minister was right. If you and your husband go about the business of becoming the right marriage partner, happiness will be the byproduct for both of you. The problem is that most people marry with the expectation that their spouse is going to be the one to bring them eternal love and happiness. This radical idea of taking responsibility for becoming the best marriage partner you can be never even occurs to most people when they marry.

How about you? Did you go into your marriage expecting your husband to be your awaited knight in shining armor, assuming that you would live happily ever after? If so, I'd like to suggest to you that happiness in marriage is something both of you need to put effort into attaining and maintaining. Becoming the best partner you can be will allow you and your spouse to build that kind of happiness. This is your challenge. I ask that you embrace it, and that you invest your best resources of time, energy, and personal effort into it.

In my work with couples who are trying to fix or save their marriage, in the initial stage of our work together they usually complain and blame each other for their marital problems. I often hear them say, "Well, that's the way I am, I can't change that!" My reply to them usually is, "How well is that working for you"? The invariable answer to that question is, "Not very well." Your see, it eventually becomes clear to them that both have been expecting the other to change and make them happy!

I ask you again. How about you? Do you find yourself playing the blame game and pointing your finger at your partner? My challenge question to you is, "What are you going to do about that?" If your marriage is not working, then you (and hopefully your partner) need to take personal responsibility for improving things before it's too late.

Don't wait for him to start the process. Be the one who gets started and leads by example; you won't regret it. Be deliberate and determined, it will serve you well.

Even in the off chance that your marriage doesn't make it in the end, at least you will know that you did your best, and you will be the better for it. You owe yourself this much. Fight for what you want. If you do, there is a really good probability that your marriage will improve as you create momentum by becoming a better marriage partner, and a better person altogether.

As I mentioned before, it is very common for spouses to blame each other for the problems in their relationship, and that is human nature. But if you want to evolve beyond that rut so you can get more out of your marriage, you must do things differently. You may be familiar with the general definition of insanity in the Alcoholics Anonymous organization, which says that insanity is "doing the same thing over and over, but expecting different results."

Perhaps you have done exactly that. The fact of the matter is that, at some point, one or both partners in an unhappy marriage get sick and tired of being sick and tired. Unfortunately, way too many of them see divorce as the solution to their problems, when it should be the absolute last resort. Divorcing may solve some of your problems, but it will also create new ones and make old problems worse. The majority of couples divorce because they want to end the emotional pain, but many regret it after the fact.

Drs. John and Julie Gottman, two renowned researchers in the field of marriage relationships have found some very interesting facts through their research, which I'd like to share with you:

- There needs to be a consistent ratio of five positive interactions for each negative interaction between partners to keep a marriage healthy. This means that couples have to be constantly working on nurturing their relationship in order for it to work and be stable. It also means that when a disruption occurs in the relationship they need to work hard at generating positive interpersonal exchanges to regain a state of harmony and balance in the marriage.

- Only 5% of divorcing couples report having obtained professional help for their marriage prior to divorce. Imagine that! It appears that the majority of those who decide to divorce don't even bother to access vital professional resources that can help them save and preserve their marriage, giving up on it prematurely.

- Couples in troubled marriages who do seek professional assistance have waited an average of 6 years too long to get professional help. This is because some couples ignore their problems, or they fail to realize the severity of these challenges. Many couples consider themselves competent enough to solve their own problems, and they may try doing what they can to resolve things on their own.

It is regrettable, however, that they wait so long to avail themselves of resources that could help save their marriage when their efforts fail. Too many of them take action when it's too late to save their marriage.

- According to the Center for Disease Control and the most recent US Census the current divorce rate is as follows:

- First time marriages resulting in divorce: 41-50%
- Second time marriages resulting in divorce: 60-67%
- Third time marriages resulting in divorce: 73-74%

Beyond these sobering statistics, as a professional I can attest to the fact that divorce has a significant negative psychological and financial impact on both spouses, as well as on their children. Children of divorce are four times more likely to divorce during their lifetime, so the damage has a ripple effect for generations to come.

My intention in presenting these facts to you is not to shame you, guilt you, or in any way overwhelm you if you are considering divorce. I simply want to encourage you to take immediate action to try saving your marriage. Of course, I also recognize that the decision to fight for your marriage and avoid becoming a statistic is a very personal and important process.

You, more than anyone else, have first-hand knowledge of what being in your marriage has been like over the years. And I can assure you that repairing a marriage takes work and commitment. Yet, as you probably know from other life experiences, anything that is worth something will cost you something. So, why not give it your best effort? I promise you, you and your partner are worth it, and your children are also worth the effort.

As you contemplate this possibility I would like to make three very important recommendations to you:

1. If you are contemplating the possibility of divorce, put it on hold so that you can really focus and invest on fixing your marriage. You won't be very effective in your attempts if you have one foot in and one foot out. Your ambivalence will cause you to just go through the motions without putting your heart in it.

2. If you are considering having an affair, or are having one, whether it is a full blown affair or an emotional one, you must do yourself a favor and end it immediately. Do not make any excuses. Attempting to fix your marriage in that situation is like trying to fill a barrel that has a big hole on the bottom. It simply won't work and will only complicate matters.

   If you are having an affair you are probably already feeling so confused and split inside you that you don't know whether you are coming or going. I would venture to guess that you also feel indecisive and ambivalent, and that the duplicity in your life is causing you immense guilt and shame.

At this point in your life's journey you have a very important decision to make: either you harness the energy that is available so you can repair your marriage, or you give it to someone else. You cannot have it both ways.

Contrary to what the popular culture and media portray about the popularity and "benefits" of having an illicit extra-marital relationship, I can assure you that affairs are the single most destructive blow to a marriage. They destroy the trust, which is the foundation of a marriage. And it can be very difficult to recover from such a traumatizing betrayal. An affair can really make your marital situation a lot worse, or devastate your marriage beyond any chance of recovery.

3. If you have symptoms of any mental health condition like depression, anxiety, substance abuse, etc., you would be wise to seek some professional help to address that. Your condition may be due to organic causes, trauma from the past, excessive stress, grief, loss,

circumstances, etc. Your symptoms may also be due to your marital difficulties, or they may be the result of a combination of factors. A professional can help you identify the causes and available treatment options to resolve them.

4. Please understand that mental health issues can be the direct cause of your marital problems as well, or that they are at least contributing to them in some fashion. Trying to repair your marriage in such vulnerable circumstances is like attempting to run a marathon with a broken leg. Taking care of yourself first makes sense because it will set you up to succeed in your efforts to improve your marriage.

This was the case of John and Kathy, a couple in their mid-thirties who had been married for over a decade and had three lovely sons. After the birth of their first son Kathy had become disillusioned with the marriage, but decided to keep quiet, thinking that things would improve on their own.

Shortly after that she began to experience mounting stress, which she did not know how to handle. She would complain and distance from John, particularly when he decided that what they needed was "more fun" and started requesting sexual practices that she disagreed with. Kathy resented John for this and many other things.

Her disillusionment turned to depression in a matter of weeks. John found himself baffled by this new reality and tried to fix the problem with solutions that seemed logical to him, but nothing seemed to work. As was typical of the dynamics in their marriage, they tacitly made an agreement not to talk about their problems. The proverbial elephant was in the room, but neither was willing to bring it up for discussion.

In time John simply gave up and started working longer hours, which compounded Kathy's emotional distress, depression, and sense of isolation. At that point they began to "communicate" by having heated arguments that never got resolved, and within 3 years their marriage turned into a battlefield that was unbearable for all involved.

Their children, who often witnessed their fights, started to show various signs of emotional distress and behavior problems, which became another point of contention and mutual blame. Both partners felt tremendous emotional pain, and their children acted out their part as a way of coping, adding to the daily chaos.

John decided this was too much for him and began to turn his attention to other things and other people. He eventually decided that he worked too hard to be putting up with that situation, and that living with a negative wife was no longer an option for him. He started to flirt and spend more time with other females who made him feel good about himself. So he decided to divorce Kathy and marry someone else, which he promptly did.

Needless to say, Kathy's depression got worse, which made life much more difficult for everyone involved. The divorce process was long and gruelling, at which point Kathy finally resolved to get the help she needed. Fortunately, she was able to resolve her depression with professional assistance, but deeply regretted not having been more proactive when the marriage could have been saved.

That is just one example of the sad scenarios I have witnessed over the years. And I'm here to tell you that it doesn't have to be that way for you, if you are willing to act on your desire to have a healthy marriage. I can tell you that what you do right now will have a major impact on you and your family for years to come.

Having said that, let's talk about what a healthy and truly intimate marital partnership is about. It will be helpful for you to have a point of reference that can serve as a guide in your process of reinventing yourself and your marriage. This is particularly important if you did not experience your parents relating to each other in a healthy and loving manner. In that type of union there are the following elements:

- Love
- Honesty

- Respect
- Intimacy
- Trust
- Faithfulness
- Safety
- Passion
- Friendship
- Appreciation
- Interdependence
- Commitment
- Responsibility
- Acceptance
- Collaboration
- Growth
- Hope
- Vision
- Contribution
- Support
- Accountability
- Vulnerability
- Empathy
- Closeness
- Sharing
- Freedom
- Reliability
- Equality
- Forgiveness
- Effective and ongoing communication

I truly believe that people go into marriage looking to experience all these things, and to make it last. I imagine that you did as well. You and your spouse may have never had some of those characteristics in your marriage, or you may have had them prior, but somehow you lost them along the way. Either way, whether you want to create these qualities in your marriage for the first time, or want to bring them back, this can become your new quest in life.

Now I want you to also consider the possibility that your marriage can serve as a transformational process that can grant you the once in a lifetime opportunity for evolving and becoming the best person you can be, and to do it in the company of your soul mate. No other relationship can offer you such a unique opportunity. Your marital relationship can actually help you grow and become the kind of person you want and need to be.

It's true, your marriage can truly be the crucible in which you mature and reach your greatest potential. In marriage you can learn to love and be loved deeply. You will also be able to know your partner and be known by him intimately, as well as experience lasting fulfillment, meaning, and purpose in life.

I could almost hear you say, "That's it! That's what I want! But where do I start?" My answer to you is, "At the beginning." Positive change needs to start with you because you have full domain over yourself. As I mentioned before, most partners exercise their personal power in trying to change each other, and this does not work. Contrary to what you may have experienced in your marriage so far, building a strong and healthy marriage is not impossible, and you have the power to do your part in making that happen.

Remember that this will be a dual process where you and your husband will be required not only to maintain the good aspects of your marriage that are already there, but to work on improving the things that prevent you from having the loving connection you are yearning for. My hope is that this book helps you to achieve both of these.

If your partner wants to join you in this journey of fixing your marriage, that is great. But if he doesn't, don't let that discourage you. The majority of the time both partners are not on the same page about their marital problems and whether there is a need for improvement. If this is the case, don't try to force him. If you do, he will react as if you were trying to shove medicine down his throat, and he will resist tooth and nail. I am sure you have tried that, only to realize that it does not work, or that it actually makes things worse.

Of course, the ideal situation would be one where both partners make a commitment to work on improving their marriage. In that scenario each would start by taking an honest look at themselves, and accepting responsibility for how they are contributing to the problems in the relationship. The next step would involve each doing the work of becoming the right kind of partner to make the marriage successful. If your partner isn't there with you, have hope because you never know, he may come along as he sees you take the lead in this important endeavor.

Let me reiterate, if your partner is not interested, or does not want to cooperate, don't let that stop you. You can still commit to your own process of self-improvement. As I said before, the "power of one" can create great momentum toward your desired outcome. I know this is possible because I have helped many courageous people who had to do this on their own.

Let me describe the typical scenario I've seen. As the concerned partner gets the process started, usually, their absent partner would become so curious about the positive changes they were noticing in their spouse, that they begin to wonder what is going on. In time they may inquire about this, and even start attending joint therapy sessions to find out what is happening. Funny thing, usually these are the partners who don't want the sessions to end, as they recognize how beneficial they are for creating a better marriage.

What do you suppose happened? Plain and simple, these individuals were led by example. As their partners improved, they were able to experience them in a way that inspired and influenced them. Your positive change can motivate your partner to come along in the process of repairing the marriage.

For example, your partner may at some point notice that you are more approachable, open, appreciative, or kind toward him. He may in turn decide to emulate your behavior and make improvements in the same areas. Before you know it, a synergistic effect takes place, creating additional momentum.

So again, I say that your need to start with yourself. Committing to our own self-improvement is as important as your commitment to your marriage. You may want to think of it in terms of making a good investment on yourself, which can pay large dividends in your future. In the end, you will be glad that you took corrective action instead of settling for less than what you want regarding the most important relationship in your life.

SELF-LOVE AND COMPASSION

This is a very important topic because many good people are great at giving the best they have to offer to others, but they can be very selfish toward themselves. This is usually because they have low self-worth, which they developed during their formative years.

Their sense of unworthiness causes them to seek love and approval by giving to others indiscriminately. They don't consider themselves worthy of love and respect, and they perceive themselves as defective, unlovable, or inadequate.

Some of these folks also develop perfectionistic tendencies, which are manifested by the compulsive need to seek acceptance from others. Their way of bonding with other people is based on performing good deeds, while appearing to be perfect in their eyes.

These individuals were raised in homes where one or both parents were critical, demanding, negative, rigid, angry, authoritarian, neglectful, uncaring, punitive, overprotective, or abusive. Such early experiences can have a negative impact on the development of the child's self-concept and belief system about themselves, life in general, the world, and other people.

This mindset of unworthiness can also occur when well-meaning parents put undue pressure on their children to be "their best" beyond what is reasonable and appropriate, based on the needs of the parents, not necessarily those of the child. For example, some parents push their kids to high levels of performance in order for their children to make them look good in the eyes of the world, or to live vicariously through their offspring.

These children grow up with a performance mentality that causes them to be people pleasers. They love, respect, give, forgive, acquiesce, meet needs, and sacrifice, believing that others deserve all those things, but they have a very difficult time receiving or expecting the same from anyone.

If you identify with any of this, please know that my intention is not to bash your parents because doing so is really unproductive. My intention is to help you gain a better understanding of the possible underlying causes for not valuing yourself as you value others. Trust me, if you don't love and value yourself, others won't either. And you will very likely attract people who take advantage of you and treat you poorly.

If this is your case, I can tell you that one of your main tasks is going to be that you learn to love yourself in order to know how to love others well, striking an appropriate balance between the two.

If you were raised in a home where you learned not to esteem yourself, your emotional wounds may have instead turned you into an individual who treats others poorly. You may be guilty of perpetrating the same offenses that were committed against you while you were growing up. Deep down inside you may feel disappointed, cynical, negative, or angry with yourself and with others.

You may have developed the tendency to be judgmental or critical of everyone around you, particularly your partner. This characteristic is probably rooted in your own insecurity and sense of inadequacy, causing you to be intolerant of negative qualities or shortcomings you see in your partner, which you possess yourself.

For example, you may dislike or even despise your

partner's inability to exercise self-control in the area of finances, while you tend to do the same by trying to live a lifestyle beyond your means.

I want you to be aware that these relational experiences point to the emotional baggage that you (and your spouse) brought into your marriage. Everyone brings some baggage into their primary relationship, and it needs to be dealt with in the context of the marriage to develop a truly intimate and healthy connection between partners.

Many times I have worked with spouses who were experiencing difficulties in this area. When I see that partners are constantly complaining about their mate, I like to inquire as to how they are feeling about themselves. What they usually tell me is that they have been feeling crummy, frustrated with themselves, or defective in some way.

So it is always a good idea to check yourself whenever you find that you are filled with negativity toward your spouse. If you are, there is a good chance that you have also been rejecting and punishing yourself for some personal failure or flaw that you perceive within you. Sometimes this self-rejection can be so intense that it is experienced as self-hatred.

I recommend that you start paying attention to the internal dialogue or self-talk that goes on in your head.

Your thoughts will clue you as to what is going on. As a matter of fact, whether you are aware of it or not, you may be hearing the same negative talk that you heard from the people who raised you. Those wounding individuals may still be living in your head rent-free.

If this is true for you, you will need to evict those negative voices out of your head and replace them with more positive self-talk. This will help you construct a new belief system about yourself and others, as well as develop a new worldview.

The following exercise is designed to help you develop an appropriate sense of kindness toward yourself, as well as to see yourself as separate from your partner (and other people in general) As you grow your ability to exercise self-compassion, you will learn to accept all aspects of your personality, including those that are deemed to be unacceptable.

This process of self-integration will also allow you to become more empathetic and accepting of others, warts and all. Furthermore, this practice can help reduce any excessive need to be accepted, needed, desired, or validated by other people.

As you engage in this ongoing process you will begin to uncover themes and patterns of thought, emotions, and behavior which are causing you emotional distress. Once you become aware of these you can begin to replace them with more positive ones.

I suggest that you do this exercise on a regular basis to achieve maximum benefit.   You will also find it particularly helpful after you have a difficult emotional experience with your partner. This will help you cultivate the ability to love and care for yourself. You may want to journal your experiences so you can track your progress over time. With practice this way of caring for yourself will become a new habit that in time will become second nature to you.

STEP 2 – EXERCISE FOR DEVELOPING SELF-AWARENESS AND COMPASSION

1. Take 10 to 15 minutes for yourself, and start by taking some deep breaths. Notice the sensations you experience in your body as take in air, as well as when you release it.

2. Now notice how your body feels as you scan it from the top of your head down to your toes.

3. Next, focus on your thoughts and pay attention to the self-talk that goes on inside your head. Be patient, as this may take some time.

4. Now ask your yourself the following questions:

• What am I telling myself about my present situation?

- What are the feelings I am experiencing?

- What is making me feel vulnerable?

- Where, when, and with whom do I recall having experienced this before?

- What do I know about my past struggles in this area?

- How have I neglected addressing this issue and meeting my needs in this regard?

- How has this interfered with my ability to get close to the people I love?

- Have I reached out to anyone for support about this issue? Can I do that now?

- What have I done to facilitate my personal healing from this emotional wound?

- What is one thing I can commit to doing so I can resolve this concern?

- What would I do if someone else was having this kind of problem?

- How can I be compassionate toward myself in this regard?

5. At the end of this exercise take some time to engage in a self-nurturing activity of your choice.

STEP 3 – EXERCISE FOR DEVELOPING COMPASSION TOWARD OTHERS

This next exercise is for those who tend to be hard on other people, especially their partner. Practice it on a regular basis, and particularly after experiencing a difficult interaction with your mate; it will make a difference.

1. Take 10 to 15 minutes of quiet time in a comfortable place and start by taking some deep breaths. As in the prior exercise, notice the sensations you experience in your body as you breathe in and out.

2. Take a moment to scan your body from top to bottom.

3. Now focus on your thoughts and notice the self-talk that is going on in your mind.

4. Ask yourself the following questions:

- What am I telling myself about this?

- Where is my partner's vulnerability?

- Am I rejecting, dismissing, or minimizing the needs and concerns of my partner?

- Have I hurt my partner with my criticism, poor attitude, put downs, ridicule, or sarcasm?

- How would I feel if I were in his shoes?

- Do I tend to be more compassionate and gracious with others than with those who are closest to me?

- Have I taken the time to express loving concern about these issues to my partner?

- Have I tried to extend myself in any way to help my partner heal in this regard?

5. After completing the exercise take some time to engage in a reparative action to resolve the disruption in your relationship with your partner. You may want to apologize, express regret, make amends, or share with your partner what you have learned by doing this exercise.

LOVE: LIFE'S QUEST

Humans are social beings made for relationship. From the early days in our mother's womb we begin the journey of being in a loving connection with "another."

From the moment we are born we begin to form attachments with our mother, father, siblings, extended family, friends, and others. This is essential for our physical and psychological survival.

Human beings are created in relationship and seek after meaningful and fulfilling connections. We experience relationships in our family of origin and home, and in many other settings while growing up. When we finally reach adulthood we seek to form permanent and intimate relationships in a home of our own when we marry and have children. These relationships constitute our primary network of interconnectedness and support.

This need for connection is the reason why very few people remain single. It's also the reason why people who divorce go on to give marriage another try, despite their hurt and disappointment. This need for emotional bonding and long lasting attachment with others is a crucial aspect of human existence. It is one of the major developmental tasks throughout the life span, and it has a very significant impact on our overall wellbeing.

The creation of attachment through marriage has played a very important role in societies through time, across cultures, and from generation to generation. Marriage is central to having social stability, emotional connection, meaning, and purpose in life. It fulfills our need for love, identity, affiliation, and belonging, which are basic human needs. Marriage and family are also the main contexts in which individuals are nurtured, cared for, and protected as they strive to reach their potential in life.

MARRIAGE AS A JOURNEY

Love in marriage is an experience with a purpose. The journey begins with "falling in love." The romance that creates attachment between husband and wife is only the beginning of the progression toward achieving deep and meaningful intimacy and connection. This stage of the relationship usually brings out the best in each partner.

Think back to the early days of your relationship with your beloved. Do you remember how exciting it was to be in love with him? You may remember that your physical senses came alive with excitement, causing you to feel energized, on top of the world, and incredibly happy. For the majority of people falling in love tends to be the ultimate life experience.

It's easy to tell that someone is in love because they seem to have a glow about them that is unmistakable. This rightful beginning allows partners to develop a strong attachment that seeks satisfaction, permanency, and commitment.

At some point while dating your partner you probably said to yourself, "This is the one!" You may remember being drawn to him, longing for his presence, and desiring to get emotionally closer to him. In time both of you decided that you had to be with each other permanently.

Partners get so caught up in this state of bliss where their needs, dreams, and expectations seem to be finally met, that they assume their life together will always be so. Each brings out the best in the other, they agree about many things, they fulfill each other's desires, they enjoy each other, and the future looks very promising.

In the midst of this delightful scenario both partners go into marriage expecting the other to make them eternally happy. They don't even think to discuss these important expectations prior to saying "I do." They just assume that their love will last forever with little or no effort on their part.

The founders of Imago Therapy, Dr. Harville Hendrix, and Dr. Helen LaKelly Hunt postulate that the relationship between marriage partners goes through developmental stages, much like a newborn does. Initially, the complete attachment and dependency necessary to create a strong emotional bond is formed. Later on the need to regain some independence and individuality within the context of the relationship gradually surfaces.

This need for connection and autonomy is very similar to what happens between a baby and his mother. He initially bonds strongly with her. After a few months he starts crawling and walking, trying to be more independent, yet wanting to be connected to his mother at the same time. Success at this stage allows for connection and autonomy simultaneously.

The same is true of marital relationships. If the couple adapts well through this developmental stage of the marriage, they gradually transition into the last stage of development, where a healthy and balanced blend of connection, interdependence, and personal autonomy is achieved. This is usually not a seamless process, but over time the relationship becomes stronger, the connection gets deeper, and the level of satisfaction increases as the couple is able to maintain the momentum in the process of becoming "soul mates."

Contrary to beliefs that are often portrayed in the arts, movies and fairy tales so popular in our culture, marriage is very rarely an effortless process or a smooth progression toward permanent bliss. Conflict happens. Conflict is meant to happen. Consider the fact that you and your partner are two different individuals trying to blend your worlds, and create a new one that is distinct from both of you, yet has elements of both of you at the same time.

The sacred space between the two of you is a living entity where the "us" happens. Caring for this entity is no easy task, but it is certainly worth your every effort. The most important thing you need to know about conflict in your marriage is that if you learn to embrace it and work through it, both of you will have the opportunity to grow as individuals, and as marriage partners.

Imago Theory maintains that conflict begins to surface after the romantic phase of the relationship has allowed partners to create attachment between them. I call this attachment the "glue" between husband and wife. It is in this middle stage where conflicts cause couples to experience the greatest difficulty, threatening their ability to maintain their attachment.

This is usually where most couples get lost because they lack the necessary skills for resolving conflict in ways that otherwise would strengthen their partnership. Their inability to resolve conflict constructively can definitely prevent them from reaching their full potential in marriage, and in a worst case scenario lead to divorce.

You may be there right now. The conflicts with your spouse simply don't get resolved, causing increasing marital distress, frustration, hurt, loss of hope, emotional distancing, disillusionment, as well as other negative experiences. You may have noticed that these unresolved conflicts and feelings tend to resurface with greater frequency and intensity as time goes by.

Couples in this situation usually tell me that they argue or fight about "stupid things", and much of the time they don't even remember exactly what the argument was about. But they know that they were not able to resolve anything. I tell them that this is because the immediate problem is not really the problem. The real problem lies underneath. Like these couples who don't know what is going on or what to do about this, you and your mate may have decided to either avoid these problems, or to argue incessantly about the same things over and over, never reaching a satisfactory solution to the conflicts you face.

If this troublesome scenario is familiar to you and your partner, both of you are probably experiencing chronic marital dissatisfaction and feeling emotionally disconnected from each other. The need for self-preservation will cause both of you to disengage in an effort to avoid experiencing greater emotional pain on an ongoing basis. Chances are that many of your arguments are directly related to the angst you may be experiencing because of the loss of the emotional connection between you.

Imago Theory also maintains that when there is distress and chronic relational disruptions between partners, the very characteristics that initially attracted them to each other begin to be perceived as irritating liabilities. For example, when you fell in love with your spouse you may have found his cool and quiet demeanor to be very attractive. At that point you may have perceived him as wise, reserved, and in control of himself. Now you may perceive him as cold, distant, uncaring, and self-absorbed.

Or you initially may have perceived his sense of humor as light hearted fun, but now you think it is silly and immature behavior. If he passionately pursued you for affection and sex in the beginning of your relationship, which was something that you could not resist back then, now when he pursues you he seems needy, clingy and pitiful. Neither of you can explain what happened, but one thing you know for sure is that your marriage is in a downward spiral of decline.

If this remains so, in time the emotional distress can become so intensely painful, that divorce may appear to be the only viable option to end the pain. Does any of this sound familiar to you? If it does, I can tell you from my years as a marriage therapist that the emotional pain you are experiencing is a normal and common reaction to your unfortunate circumstances.

And I can also tell you that there is hope for you and your marriage. Your current situation is not as good as it gets. There is more, a lot more that you can experience in your marriage. Repairing your marriage is not going to happen overnight, however. I tell couples to think about how long it took for their marriage to reach its current state so that they realize that they need to be patient with themselves and each other. Re-inventing or repairing a marriage takes time.

I encourage you to continue following the steps in this book so that you can create and have more than what you have in your marriage right now. Be realistic and hopeful at the same time. Remain committed to yourself, to your partner, and to this process. I can tell you that the possibilities are endless.

EXTROVERTS AND INTROVERTS

I am sure you have heard these terms before, but probably not in relation to marriage or dating. This is an important topic to discuss because you and your partner need to understand how your basic temperament influences your relationship.

Extroverts are individuals whose personality tends to be overtly expressive. They are outgoing and sociable. They readily know what they are thinking and feeling, and are able to articulate their thoughts and feelings with ease. I like to say that extroverts are like microwave ovens; they are ready in a jiffy.

As a matter of fact, extroverts by nature are able to process their thoughts and feelings by talking or expressing themselves in some fashion. No one has to ask extroverts about what they are thinking or feeling because they offer it without being prompted. Their energy is directed outwardly, and they tend to be the ones who pursue or initiate what they want to see happen in their relationships, particularly when it comes to their marriage.

If you are an extrovert, you probably like to express affection, enjoy discussing things in detail with your partner, and initiate conversations or interactions with others. You may like social events and seek out your partner and other relationships because you thrive in the company of other people. You also like resolving conflicts right away, usually by talking or by doing something. Some extroverts may talk excessively, especially when they experience emotional distress, sometimes overwhelming or "flooding" their partner.

Introverts, on the other hand, are individuals who tend to be reserved, are laid back, enjoy being alone, and prefer less socialization. They need to process their thoughts and feelings internally, and they like taking their time to do so. If you ask them what they are thinking or feeling, they would tell you that they don't know what they are thinking or feeling at the moment. They'd also say they need to think about it before they can venture communicating these things to you or anyone else.

Their energy is directed inwardly, and they learn by observing and listening. Introverts are usually easy going individuals who do not like to attract attention to themselves or be in the limelight. They enjoy solitude and want privacy. Introverts also tend to take information from their surroundings to process it internally, and they like to take their time to "digest" the information.

I like to think of introverts as crock-pots; they like to simmer plenty of time, and you cannot rush them. Introverts are happy to let others initiate interactions or pursue them in relationship, particularly in their own marriage.

If you are an introvert, you are probably a person of few words, rarely volunteering to talk about your feelings, as you may consider them to be a private matter. You are likely content with talking only when necessary or when prompted, and you enjoy spending time at home or in a quiet setting. You often let go of potential conflicts, and when you experience emotional distress you get particularly quiet, even close off or shut down to avoid feeling overwhelmed by your partner.

Extroversion and introversion is a continuum, and people fall somewhere in that gamut. Very few individuals are on one extreme or the other. Please understand that these basic personality types are just different, not defective or inadequate in any way.

What is interesting is that introverts and extroverts tend to attract each other. So, it is really true that opposites attract, like the yin and yang. Every couple I have ever helped over the years has been a combination of an extrovert and an introvert. I believe that this can make a marriage interesting and fun if the couple learns to appreciate their differences, allowing them to create diversity that enriches their relationship.

In marriage extroverts tend to be "maximizers" who amplify things, particularly when upset. One of my Imago colleagues says that they are like an octopus. Their lovely tentacles are out there feeling things out and pursuing their partner, which may cause them to over-function in the relationship.

When extroverts perceive conflict or trouble in their marriage their pursuit usually intensifies, wanting to talk and connect with their mate immediately. They have two things in mind: they want to resolve conflicts right away, as well as reduce the emotional tension they are experiencing internally because of the conflict.

Their intense pursuit can overwhelm their introverted counterpart, who tends to be more like a turtle. Introverts tend to be "minimizers" who play things down, dismiss them, or ignore them altogether. This may cause them to under-function in their marriage.

When pursued intensely by an upset partner, introverts go inside their protective shell and hide. And they won't venture coming out until their pursuer gets quiet or goes away for good. Afterward it will take them some time to process what happened in their relationship, particularly once they've become overwhelmed or upset to the point of shutting down.

Unfortunately, these basic differences in temperament can cause marriage partners major trouble. Most couples do not understand these important differences, and they lack the necessary skills that can help them communicate and resolve conflicts effectively. When partners learn about each other and work together to develop relational skills that embrace their differences, satisfaction in marriage is quite possible for both spouses.

The skills presented in the following chapters of this book will help introverted and extroverted partners find a happy medium where they can nurture and negotiate their relationship, as well as to maintain a healthy balance in their partnership.

Introverts can function effectively in the marriage by learning how to initiate, respond, pursue, express, and participate in the relationship. Extroverts can do the same by learning to regulate their emotions, conserve their energy, relax, pace their interactions, and allow their mate to participate in the marriage.

CHAPTER 2: YOUR BRAIN IS YOUR LOVE ORGAN

"Your brain controls everything you do, feel, and think."
Dr. Daniel Amen

Your brain is the most marvelous thing in all of creation, and your best resource for creating a loving marriage. You can train your brain to function in ways that nurture your relationships, particularly your marriage. There is a saying in the field of Neuroscience, which says that "neurons that fire together wire together." These amazing brain cells connect with each other to produce vast and complex networks that determine how we think, how we feel, and how we act.

Scientists used to think that those brain networks could not be changed, but recent Neurobiology research has shown that those networks can be changed, and new networks can be created as we engage in new ways of thinking, feeling, and behaving. This is an amazing concept and a wonderful reality that you can take advantage of in the process of creating the relationship of your dreams.

As far as your marital situation is concerned, you need to know that just because things have deteriorated in your relationship due to negative thinking, painful emotions, and poor behavior; it does not have to continue to be this way. And it certainly does not mean that your marriage has to end.

Indeed, you can begin to turn things around, and your brain is your best ally to make this happen. But you need to make the important decision to make changes that can help "rewire" your brain as you learn to love intentionally.

This means that you must be deliberate and consistent in your approach to healing and re-inventing your marriage. Not only that, but you (and hopefully your husband) will learn to do things differently until you develop new patterns of interaction. Over time the dynamics (the forces that produce activity and change) between the two of you will improve. This, in turn, will create additional new patterns of interaction that in time will redefine your relationship and encourage more growth.

The human brain plays a very important role in falling in love and staying in love. Researchers have found that in the beginning of a relationship, when a couple starts experiencing attraction toward each other, their brains begin to produce a cocktail of "feel-good" hormones which allow them to form the attachment and connection of romantic love.

This cocktail of hormones is very powerful, as it produces happy feelings of bonding and excitement that are unique to falling in love. According to social psychologist and leading researcher in the area of love and relationships, Dr. Ellen Berscheid, in this blissful state smitten lovers tend to idealize their partner, magnifying their virtues and minimizing or ignoring their negative traits or behavior.

These friendly hormones were responsible for the two of you wanting to perpetuate that initial blissful state, which eventually led you to marry. In time, however, once the commitment was made, your brain's production of those hormones gradually returned to normal levels. At that point your marriage may have started to feel less exciting, and greater effort was probably needed to maintain the connection with your partner.

During this challenging phase the majority of couples start to feel some disappointment, boredom, and even resentment toward each other, as they realize that their needs and expectations are not being met. Interestingly enough, at the same time conflict begins to emerge as both partners start to really notice each other's flaws and quirks.

Do you recall this happening to you and your partner? You may have thought to yourself, "This is not what I signed up for!", or "This is not how I imagined it would be!" The interesting thing is, your partner was probably thinking the same way. So I imagine that both of you began to struggle with the new reality that your marriage was not what you hoped for, or desired.

Not knowing what to do, you may have resorted to

tactics like protesting, complaining, distancing, arguing, blaming, manipulating, or criticizing each other in an effort to try to regain the blissful love you once shared.

But as you know all too well, this has not helped to bring the love back, or if it did, it probably lasted only for a brief moment. You and your partner may have panicked, thinking that you made a mistake in marrying. Trust me, if you started over and fell in love with someone new, you would experience the exact same process.

So, the bottom line reality is that your level of satisfaction in your relationship has gradually decreased, and your disappointment and frustration has increased. You may even think that you have exhausted everything you knew to do to fix it. Another possible scenario would be one where your partner is clueless as to what is going on. He may think that all is well in the relationship, and this probably makes you feel alone and confused, wondering whether your perception of reality is accurate.

Now you find yourself at a loss for what to do next. You may feel frustrated or desperate at this point. Do not despair because there is a lot more that you can do. As you carry out the steps outlined in this book, you will discover that when you do things that actually work, you are rewarded for investing on the most important relationship of your life. You will be glad you did.

One of the most exciting findings in the field of Neuroscience is the fact that when two people are in relationship, their brains "regulate" and influence each other. Isn't that amazing? That is why when your partner comes home in a bad mood, after a while you follow suit and get in a bad mood yourself.

Why is it important for you to know this? It's because you can use this brain regulation effect to your advantage. As you start to display a more positive attitude toward your partner, engage in connecting activities, or express love, there is a really good chance that he will respond in kind.

Do not give up if he doesn't respond immediately. There will be times when you will be tempted to do just that. Have faith because it may take time for him to warm up and start opening up to you. Sometimes it is difficult for both partners to trust that those positive changes will last. One or both of you may expect "the other shoe to drop", so to speak.

To illustrate this important fact, let me tell you about my work with a woman who had decided to divorce as a way of ending the painful conflict in her marriage. As we talked she decided to give her marriage one last chance, and she postponed filing for divorce. She began to work on improving her thoughts, feelings, and behavior toward her husband.

A couple of weeks into the process her husband came with her just to tell me that I shouldn't even dream of changing him (funny he should say that since I had not even met him before) He also wanted me to tell him exactly what I was doing to make his wife be so nice!

As time went by he would invite himself to our sessions, just so he could find out what was going on, he said. He found himself participating more and more, and his own behavior and attitude gradually improved over time. When the therapy was about to conclude, he was the one who did not want it to end! Needless to say, there was no divorce, and their marriage was saved.

And then there was the woman who bitterly complained that her husband simply wouldn't talk to her. This made her feel terribly lonely in the marriage. It also made her furious because when they were dating they were able to talk about "anything and everything" for hours. But the mounting conflict and distress in their relationship caused her husband to shut down every time she tried to talk to him.

This made her even more furious and anxious, which caused her to pursue him relentlessly in a desperate effort to connect with him. He perceived her efforts as a control tactic that overwhelmed him each time, and one that he had to avoid at any cost. The only thing he could do is distance some more, just so he could feel safe. It was like the dog chasing his own tail, an endless vicious cycle that was ruining their marriage.

At the beginning of our work together he reluctantly participated in discussions, but in time he opened up to the point where I had a hard time keeping him quiet! He'd say to his wife, "Boy, being here is so nice, I really do like talking, I just didn't know it."

This reluctant man learned to communicate with his wife and deal effectively with conflicts in their marriage because she learned how to engage him appropriately. Instead of resorting to criticism, complaints, accusations, or blame, this smart woman developed the ability to approach him in a manner that was inviting and respectful. He in turn learned to respond and initiate interactions instead of shutting her out.

The exercises that I provide in this book are what I call "re-constructive experiences" that can help re-invent you and your marriage. They are personal investments that can help you become the kind of person and spouse that you want to be. As you do the exercises you will be able to reap benefits that can put your marriage on a better course, making a difference for you and for your partner.

These practices can also allow both of you to experience individual and collective healing from past emotional wounds through the process of participating in this exciting journey toward creating the love you yearn for. Again, remember to be patient. These changes do not happen overnight. Establishing new patterns, dynamics, and healing in your marriage will take time. It is almost as if you and your husband were to start dating again. You get the chance to fall in love twice.

I could not write this book without discussing in more detail the crucial importance of early relationships, namely, those with our primary caregivers (usually mother and father) So, let me reiterate that I am not in favor of parent bashing because it is a useless endeavor that will not help you.

When I bring up family of origin issues my goal is to help you gain awareness so you can understand how the experiences you had in important relationships early on in your life have impacted your relational ability. This discussion, therefore, is about getting to know yourself better, and to understand why you function in relationship the way you do.

The most important thing for you to know about this topic is that the essence and quality of your relationship with your parents is the single most impactful factor in your style of relating to others, particularly you partner. Even if your relationship history includes a parent who was physically or emotionally absent from your life, I can assure you that this very fact has played a significant role in how you show up, or fail to show up in your relationship with your partner.

You may be asking yourself, "And what does all this have to do with me and my marriage?" I can only say to you that it has everything to do with both. Your relational style, which you developed in your early relationship (or lack thereof with your parents) is the backbone or foundation for how you operate in your relationships, particularly with your husband.

Your manner of relating to others was formed long before he came along. It was developed based on the quality and strength of the bond or attachment between you and your parents or primary caregivers, starting in infancy.

Dr. Luis Cozolino, a psychologist and researcher in the field of Neuroscience says that the relationship we have with our mother and father has a huge impact on how the nervous system develops, and that this is due to the fact that early childhood is a period where massive brain development takes place.

This is how the cumulative experiences and interactions with your parents became experiential markers which you internalized as a mental and emotional model for relating to others. Throughout life this framework is used by your brain for processing information, as well as for creating meaning out of your experiences in relationship.

This framework greatly determines what you believe, how you think, how you feel emotionally, how you act, and how you show up in relationships, particularly in your relationship with your mate.

Furthermore, recent studies in Neuroscience have also demonstrated that early interpersonal experiences with primary caregivers determine how the human brain develops its physical and biochemical structure, which is transmitted genetically from generation to generation.

If your relationship with your parents made you feel consistently safe, loved, nurtured, cared for, and emotionally connected when you were growing up, you learned that being in relationship with others is a desirable experience that enriches your life, generates positive feelings in you, and brings meaning to your existence. This would allow you to relate well to others, seek connection with them, and maintain meaningful and long lasting relationships.

If, on the other hand, this important process was disrupted, chaotic, or hurtful, your relational ability would be affected negatively, interfering with the development of trust, identity, safety, self-worth, and meaningful connection with others.

You may have learned to be fearful of emotional intimacy and consequently have learned to avoid it. Or you may feel emotionally vulnerable, causing you to lack authenticity with others. You may have learned to protect yourself by being domineering, distrustful, controlling, critical, negative, abusive, or rejecting of others in general.

Your brain started to build memories through those early experiences from the moment you were born. Research shows that two hormones in particular are critically important in the bonding process between an infant and her mother. These also facilitate the formation of social memories, affiliation behaviors, as well as acquiring the ability to learn, manage emotions, and make decisions.

These cumulative experiences and their "flavor" are stored in your memory long before you acquire the ability to use language. This is why you can't recall memories from your early years. Without language, you are not able to consciously recall such experiences, but your sub-conscious mind and your body sure have a record of these. Those pre-linguistic memories unconsciously show up as feelings, reactions, and defense mechanisms.

As I said before, memories, whether they are consciously recalled or not, are a key factor in the development of one's ability to regulate emotions and respond to stimuli that is encountered in various situations, particularly in regard to social interactions. In other words, social memory is a very important part of the programming system of the marvelous computer that is your brain.

This "operating system" runs your brain 24 hours a day, 7 days a week for your entire life. Like the software in your computer, you don't even realize it's there, but it is running all the time. This complex system contains the beliefs that you hold about yourself, the world, other people, and situations. It generates the thoughts that pop into your head. These thoughts in turn determine how you feel emotionally, and your feelings shape your behavior.

Your behavior then loops back to reinforce the beliefs that you already have. Patterns of thinking, feeling, and behaving are established and maintained in this way. These patterns also contain a personal narrative or self-talk which serves as your point of reference or mindset for how you function in the context of relationship.

For example, if your parents didn't allow you to express anger while growing up, you may have learned that expressing anger was not a good thing. So you were conditioned to keep your angry feelings inside. You may have also experienced rejection by them when you did get angry, so you learned that you were accepted only when "being nice." So you came to believe that it is wrong to experience angry feelings, that you have no right to express your anger, and perhaps that there is even something wrong with you.

This is particularly true of women. In many cultures women are socialized to be "lady-like", and they learn that "nice girls" are not supposed get mad. So you may have learned to smile when you were annoyed, frustrated, miffed, or downright mad. And there is a really good chance that you brought this mindset and pattern into your relationships, and especially into your marriage. Furthermore, you probably married someone who also doesn't like it when you get angry and expects you to "be nice" all the time.

In summary, the overall quality of the interpersonal relationship you had with your parents while growing up had an imprinting effect which determines your style of attachment to others. It also defines your relational ability, particularly in regard to your marriage.

The good news is that if things did not go well for you in this area while growing up you can intentionally create "reconstructive experiences" in your current intimate relationship with your husband, which can help rewire your brain and improve your marriage. In this way you can gain the ability to create a genuine and satisfying relationship. I would say that everyone can use some help in this area. We all have relationship issues to resolve, simply because we were raised by imperfect people.

Part of your personal responsibility as an adult entails making the necessary repairs that your "unfinished business" requires. Don't settle for playing the blame game in your relationship. This will only paralyze you and cause you to feel like a victim. It will rob you of the opportunities you have in the present to create a healthy marriage, which is what you really want, isn't it?

The truth is that as a child you didn't have a choice about many things. You couldn't pick another set of parents, move out, support yourself, or exercise the power to make important decisions. As an adult, however, you have the power to make important changes. Unless you make a conscious decision to re-invent yourself, you will continue to recreate the past by following the same old patterns. You have the opportunity now to create a new reality and more functional patterns that work for you.

You can think of this process as the healing path that will help you develop a new brain. Imagine that! I think this is exciting and it ought to give you hope. Such a process will allow you to develop greater self-awareness, as well as awareness of others.

You will be able to see the world both from your own perspective, as well as from your partner's perspective. It will also allow you to be more flexible and mindful. You will be able to take in the thoughts, feelings, perceptions, beliefs, and motives of other people. It will make you less emotionally reactive and you will enjoy a greater sense of overall emotional wellbeing.

I recall the story of John, an intelligent man in his mid-thirties, who grew up with a very self-centered single mother who thought that the world revolved around her. He told me that no matter what the topic of conversation was, she always made herself the center of attention.

She never encouraged him to make even simple decisions, have an opinion, or express his needs or feelings. John recalled that no matter how hard he worked at accomplishing something, she always took credit for it. She liked saying that she was the one who created his success, and of course, he owed her for that.

Not having a father as a role model in his life, early on John learned to please his mother, mainly to avoid her anger and manipulation. As an adult he married a woman named Sandra, who had a very similar personality and sense of self-absorption as his mother. When they disagreed, she always managed to have the upper hand. Being an introverted individual, and based on his prior experiences with his mother, John let his wife have her way, establishing the same dynamic as with his mother.

At first Sandra liked this because it put her in a position of power and control in the marriage. In time, however, she started to interpret John's acquiescence as a sign of weakness, and loathed him for "not being a man", which she often told him with disdain. Later on she began blaming him for all her unhappiness. John simply ignored her. After several years she met a man she thought was her long lost soul mate, had an affair with him, and eventually left John for her new love interest.

In my work to help John recover from the betrayal and painful rejection he experienced, he was able to gain a conscious understanding of the source of his chronic anxiety, poor self-esteem, avoidant behavior, and lack of ability to make decisions. As he practiced the exercises I assigned him to do, those experiences gave him an opportunity to reflect on his anxious and insecure attachment to his mother. John became aware that he had learned a style of relating to others based on what he experienced with her.

He was also able to deal with his fear of rejection, which caused him to be an avoidant doormat in his relationships with women his entire life. Those times of reflection, along with other reconstructive experiences were key for him. John learned to be more assertive, which is what helped him create a new paradigm for relating to others.

He felt liberated and healed. He was able to realize that he was indeed the most important agent in his own adult life, and that he had the power to create and maintain healthy relationships with others. He became a happier man.

Research in Neuroscience has shown that the human brain contains primitive parts called the "lower brain", whose main function is to ensure your physical and psychological survival. They also store those emotional pre-linguistic memories that you cannot remember consciously, which I talked about earlier. These brain structures comprise your emotional core and are busy constantly scanning the environment to assess whether there is safety or danger in your environment.

These primitive structures cause you to avoid or fight what you perceive as dangerous, whether the danger is real or imagined. They are also involved with your physical and emotional survival. When you go into survival mode all bets are off. You may say and do things that you wouldn't under normal circumstances.

The human brain also contains more evolved parts called the "upper brain", which are involved with impulse control, reflection, planning, abstract thinking, decision-making, reasoning, intentional behavior, problem-solving, and logic. These sophisticated parts of your brain allow you to be aware of your thoughts and feelings, think rationally, control your impulses, and be able to behave in appropriate ways with your partner.

The upper and lower parts of the human brain have pathways that connect them and serve as feedback mechanisms. These brain structures can also activate different parts of your nervous system in the rest of your body, much like the accelerator and brake pedals in your vehicle.

When you perceive a threat, the lower brain activates the accelerator, generating a reaction (or over-reaction) facilitated by stress hormones. In this state you are in reactive mode. When you perceive safety, the brake is engaged, causing you to be calm and relaxed. In this state of homeostasis you are quite able to respond appropriately to situations.

A bit more good news for you is the fact that your nervous system has a third branch, which is called the vagus nerve. It is connected to your heart, other major organs, and your abdomen. Its main function is to send sensory information about the state of your body, particularly your gut, to your brain. This is why we have the popular saying, "trust your gut", as this part of your nervous system gathers and communicates to your brain important intuitive sensory information in a feedback fashion.

Your vagus nerve is very much involved when it comes to relationships because it facilitates social functioning. It allows you to be gracious, especially when under pressure, because it helps you to control the automatic reactions from your body, as when your spouse or your boss do or say something you don't like.

I recall a recent situation where my husband and I were provoked by someone we had helped in many ways. I heard this ungrateful man questioning my husband in a manner which suggested that we had cheated him in the process of giving him and his entire family vital assistance.

This was so terribly unfair, untrue, and inappropriate, that reactively at first I wanted to lash out at this man and throw him out of our home, ordering him to never come back. But I knew better than to do such a thing. I started to breathe slowly and deeply, letting my mind and body work together to keep calm and respond in an appropriate manner.

Thank goodness for my friendly vagus nerve (and my gracious husband's), which helped both of us to refrain from mistreating this individual. We handled the situation in the most appropriate and respectful way. In time we decided to let go of the relationship.

In order to turn your brain into your best ally in developing your ability to create and maintain good relationships, you need to do some integrative work. This will allow the various parts of your brain and nervous system to work together for your benefit.

The key is engaging in practices that will serve to strengthen the more evolved parts of your brain so they can regulate the more primitive parts of your brain. In this manner you will create strong neural networks and feedback mechanisms that allow you to respond to people and situations, instead of overreacting. The exercises that follow will help you with this.

STEP 4 - EXERCISE FOR DEVELOPING PERSONAL AWARENESS

This mindfulness exercise is designed to help raise your

level of awareness of your bodily sensations so you can learn to soothe your nervous system when there is emotional reactivity.

1. Sit on a comfortable chair where your back is supported and your feet are touching the ground. Your hands can rest comfortably on your sides with the palms facing up.

2. Now take 3 deep cleansing breaths that reach the bottom of your lungs. You will notice that your belly rises when you breathe this way.

3. Let your breathing return to its natural rhythm and simply start noticing the physical sensations associated with your breath. Take time to notice the sensations you experience as the air comes in, and as you follow it until your breath is released.

    You will become aware of the freshness in the air coming in through your nostrils, the changes in the temperature of the air as it travels into your lungs, as well as when you finally release your breath.

4. Notice the effortless and rhythmic nature of your breath.

5. Notice the beating of your heart, your pulse, your belly, your muscles and joints.

6. When your mind wanders, and it will, kindly bring yourself back to noticing your breathing again. In and out, in and out, and so on.

7. Do the same if you experience a feeling and your mind starts going in that direction.

Engaging in this simple practice for 5-10 minutes a day will get you acquainted with your body. Be gentle with yourself. Practice makes perfect. If something troubling comes into your awareness while doing this exercise, make sure you engage support from a professional who can help you work through your concerns.

EMOTIONAL REGULATION

If you did not learn to manage your feelings while growing up, chances are they are controlling you and causing havoc in the process. The more primitive part of your brain is in the driver's seat, probably generating a lot of emotional conflict within yourself, as well as interpersonal conflict. The good news is that as an adult you can still develop the ability to modulate your emotions.

The following exercise is designed to help you develop the ability to manage your feelings more effectively. This practice will strengthen the more evolved part of your brain, which can aid you in modifying the automatic emotional reactions you experience.

STEP 5 - EXERCISE FOR DEVELOPING EMOTIONAL REGULATION

1. Begin this exercise by taking a moment or two to recognize the fact that you are learning to manage your feelings, sensations, and reactions in a beneficial way, and that with practice you will get better at it.

2. Start your breathing practice as described in the previous exercise, following steps 1 through 5.

3. As you continue breathing comfortably, imagine that you are looking up at the sky, and that there are clouds passing by. Those clouds are like your feelings, sensations, and emotional reactions. Like the clouds, these experiences usually come, they stay for a while, then dissipate.

    This exercise will help you learn how to recognize them, observe them, then help them dissipate.

4. Bring to mind a recent instance or moment where you experienced an intense reaction or feeling that was uncomfortable, painful, or downright overwhelming for you.

You may recall where you were, who was present, what was happening at the time, what you were saying to yourself, and what set you off.

5. Next, take the thoughts, feelings, and actions of that moment and put each into a cloud. Make sure to continue breathing comfortably.

6. Now move away from the clouds and just observe them as being outside of yourself. Do so without any self-criticism or judgment. Take more deep breaths and notice your body and mind as they gradually relax.

7. Step back farther and watch the clouds get smaller and beginning to dissipate. Continue to observe the distant clouds as you breathe with a sense of personal acceptance and relief, releasing any remaining self-judgment or tension.

You are simply witnessing a very interesting phenomenon that is taking place out there, way up in the sky.

You are just observing a curious event that continues to evolve with time.

Remember to continue breathing comfortably.

8. Now take some time to notice your body and how it feels to be calm at this moment in time. Notice the stillness in your mind as you attend to its present state of calmness. You can be assured that with practice, even the most difficult emotional experiences can dissipate and become softer and more manageable.

9. Be patient with this practice. As you engage in it regularly, you will become more and more skilled in generating a positive shift as you work through the triggers that you experience.

10. When you do get triggered, instead of telling yourself, "There I go again!" you can tell yourself that this gives you another useful opportunity for practicing your new skill.

HEALING EMOTIONAL WOUNDS FROM THE PAST

Every human being experiences emotional wounds while growing up. Primary caregivers are imperfect people with problems and issues of their own. Most parents try to do their best for their children under their circumstances, but they can't avoid making mistakes, despite their best intentions.

Some of them recognize their errors in parenting hindsight, and may apologize or make necessary amends for that. Others don't recognize their mistakes at all, as they are either clueless, afraid to admit their past mistakes, too proud to acknowledge these to their children, or have no idea as to how to correct things.

But your happiness and wellbeing cannot depend on, or wait for your parents to do the right thing in this regard. Perhaps your parents are deceased, too ill to deal with this sort of thing, or maybe they are cut off from your life. But as I said before, it's your personal responsibility to address and resolve these important issues for yourself.

The next exercise is more advanced than the previous ones. Before you attempt it, you need to know that you may experience emotional discomfort or intense emotional pain, particularly if you start to recall traumatic memories from the past.

Note: Make sure to stop if you get overwhelmed by the memories or emotions associated with these wounds. If this is the case, I would strongly recommend that you consult with a mental health professional who can help you work through your emotional conflicts.

STEP 6 - EXERCISE FOR HEALING EMOTIONAL WOUNDS

You will need a journal and pen for this exercise.

1. Sit in a comfortable and quiet place that affords

you privacy. You may want to light a scented candle and play soft, soothing music in the background.

2. Close your eyes and begin by doing the breathing exercise as before, noticing the sensations you experience in your body.

3. Take some time to identify a painful experience from your past. Continue breathing as you recall the details of that experience, such as where you were at the time, how you felt, how you reacted to the experience, and what you told yourself about it.

4. Focus on the people involved and how they participated or failed to participate in that experience. Allow images and symbols to come to the surface. These can be very subtle, so take your time doing this.

5. Notice your breathing once more, as well as the physical sensations you experience in your body.

6. Open your eyes and start writing down the story as if it were taking place right now. Talk about what you experience as you recall this in the here-and-now.

7. Write about the meaning of this experience for you, and how you coped with it at the time.

8. Discuss other similar experiences that had the same "flavor" or theme for you.

9. Write about how this experience shaped your development, how it impacted you emotionally, how it affected your self-esteem, as well as your opinion of the people involved.

10. Talk about how this has influenced the way you relate to your spouse, children, friends, or others in general.

11. Discuss aspects of the experience that were, or are most challenging for you.

12. What aspects of the experience have allowed you to develop specific strengths or qualities? Write about that.

13. Close your eyes again and breathe deeply, again noticing the physical sensations in your body.

14. Imagine what it would be like for this emotional wound to be healed and resolved. What would be happening? How would you feel? What personal changes would you notice? How would this affect your belief system and your way of thinking? What would your behavior be like?

15. Finally, open your eyes again and write down the

actions or specific steps you need to take to achieve healing in this regard.

What positive changes would you like to make in this area of your life in the present? Focus on the resources you have at your disposal to accomplish this. Seek professional help if necessary.

16. Finally, start taking "baby steps" by doing the things that would be easiest for you to generate positive change. Gradually start doing the more challenging ones once you start experiencing success. Be kind and patient with yourself. Remember that you are re-wiring your brain, and that is no small feat.

CHAPTER 3: LOOKING IN THE MIRROR

"The price of greatness is responsibility."
Sir Winston Churchill

As I said before, it is typical for partners to blame each other for their marital troubles. Nothing can improve as long as the blame game is being played. Things can definitely improve if you recognize that you are personally responsible for how you participate in your marriage, and that you have the power to change the way in which you contribute to its wellbeing.

I want to reiterate that trying to change your partner will only bring out more resistance and conflict, so why waste your precious time and energy doing something that does not work? Perhaps it is time that you start making good use of your time, resources, and energy to improve what you are able to.

It is very important that you realize that in marriage you are responsible FOR yourself, NOT for your partner. You are also responsible TO your partner and your marriage. This simply means that you need to focus on improving yourself to generate dynamic changes in your marriage.

Most marriage partners I see in my practice don't like to hear that because their agenda is usually to have me fix their spouse, as they have not succeeded in doing this on their own. This "pass the buck", finger pointing mentality and modus operandi reminds me of what typical politicians do. No one wants to do the hard work because they don't think the problems are their doing, but they sure expect someone else to do what they want. Like kids in a mud fight they find themselves immersed in the mess up to their necks, but unwilling to get out of the mud pit.

So, I will tell you the same thing I tell the couples I see in my practice, and that is that each of you needs to be 100% responsible for what you bring to the relational space in your marriage. In this manner you will effectively meet your responsibility for yourself, period. At the same time you will be allowing your partner to do likewise.

This is how, instead of being part of the problem, you become part of the solution. It will empower you to show up in your primary relationship in a way that honors your partner, as well as the sacred relational space you share with him. This shift can serve to inspire your spouse to follow suit. He can begin to focus his energy on making positive changes of his own instead of resisting you at every turn.

To start this important process the very first thing you need to do is take a good, honest look at yourself. Spend some time examining your own way of thinking, feeling, and acting in your marriage. I know that this can be painful, and the natural tendency is to avoid it.

I want to encourage you to press forward simply because you are worth it. Knowing that this will impact your marriage in a positive way should also incentivize you.

I suggest that you start a journal. Writing things down is cathartic, as the process will allow you to clarify your thoughts and feelings. Sometimes people behave poorly out of confusion and lack of clarity. It's as if they are on autopilot mode, not even realizing where they are going.

Journaling will help you gain clarity and coherence. Such a journal also becomes a record that can help you keep track of your progress. I would suggest that you keep your journal in a secure place if you have concerns about privacy. That way you can express yourself honestly and without fear of exposure.

STEP 7 - EXERCISE FOR TAKING PERSONAL RESPONSIBILITY

I want you to ask yourself the following questions to raise your awareness, and record your answers in your journal:

- How have I been contributing to the problems in my marriage?

- Have my expectations of my partner and marriage been realistic?

- Have I expected my partner to meet all my needs and make me happy?

- Have I blamed my partner for my failures, poor decisions, and shortcomings?

- Do I find it difficult to give or receive love?

- Where and how have I fallen short in my personal responsibility to love and care for myself?

- How well have I contributed to the wellbeing of my partner and our relationship?

- Do I express my personal needs, desires, hopes, and boundaries, in appropriate ways?

- Is it difficult for me to do so? Why is that?

- Do I expect my partner to read my mind about these things?

- Has my approach toward him about these things been appealing?

- Have I made excuses for my failure to be responsible in these areas?

- Have I experienced similar problems in other

relationships? With prior partners? With my parents? With other family members? With my friends? What consequences have I endured from those situations?

- What are the defense mechanisms I have used to protect or defend myself from hurt in my relationships?

- How have I failed to represent myself well in this marriage?

- Have I over-functioned or under-functioned in this relationship?

- What are the most important values for me as a person?

- What is most important to me in my personal life, marriage, and family?

- Have my attitude, actions, goals, priorities, and character been congruent with my values?

- What do I need to change in myself so I can bring a better "me" to the sacred space of my relationship with my spouse?

- In what ways have I neglected pursuing my dreams, passions, and goals?

- What have I done to grow and mature as a person?

- Do I make it difficult for my spouse to exhibit his best qualities? How do I do that?

- Do I make it easy for my partner to exhibit his flaws, shortcomings, and negative traits? How do I do that?

After doing this exercise I encourage you not to let the failures, hurts, and negative experiences from the past define your present reality. As a matter of fact, you can allow the past to be your greatest teacher. Learning from your errors will allow you to take corrective actions that can help you construct a new reality in the present, based on those experiences.

Please know that what you do with the lessons from your past can also prepare you for new opportunities in the present and in the future. The truth is that people learn more from adversity than from success, so glean from those experiences the wisdom that can help change the course of your life and relationships.

If you have experienced abuse, neglect, betrayal, or abandonment that have traumatized you, I urge you to get professional help so you can heal and reinvent your-self. Personal healing is very important because it is quite difficult to know how to love another person in a healthy manner if you have not learned to love and value yourself.

Experiences like that can have a very negative impact on your ability to trust as well. And without the ability to trust you will have a hard time getting close to your mate. These wounds can definitely affect the way in which you relate to him, your children, and others in general.

I want to emphasize once more that it is your personal responsibility to resolve those unresolved issues from your past because they are interfering with your present ability to be truly emotionally close and vulnerable in your relationship with your partner.

Dr. Harville Hendrix says that your relationship with your partner actually requires you to grow and stretch in the areas where growth is necessary. Therefore, your partner can be a very helpful ally in the healing process of resolving your "unfinished business" from the past, and in your growth toward maturity.

Please understand that what got broken in the context of past relationships can be healed in the context of your current relationship. In other words, your marriage can be the context in which your emotional hurts and the hurts of your partner can be healed.

People whose first marriage fails quite often marry the

same type of individual. Sigmund Freud articulated the phrase "repetition compulsion" to describe a person's tendency to re-create negative past experiences and patterns which are familiar, and saw it as pathological. Those who ascribe to this proposition would say that this is why people who grew up in abusive homes will often marry abusive partners. And if they divorce they will probably marry another abusive partner.

Other theories, by contrast, see this drive as the natural tendency of the wounded human being to re-create the familiar in the search for healing and wholeness through relationship. Proponents of these theories believe that people do so in an effort to resolve their "unfinished business" from the past. I don't know about you, but I find this more appealing and hopeful. Additionally, I have found it to be true in my work with couples time and time again.

Consider Mary and Tom, for instance. They came to see me because their marriage was on the rocks and he wanted to divorce. They had married while in the midst of a whirlwind 7 month romance that promised to be better than their failed previous marriages. This was Tom's fourth marriage, and Mary's third.

The first time we met the main question Tom had was, "Would you explain to me why it is that I keep marrying the same woman, and the only difference is that they have different names?" Mary asked herself the same question about her choice of partners. Neither could believe that they had gotten themselves into another dysfunctional relationship, despite their best intentions this time around.

In the course of our work together both partners didn't just find an explanation that helped them make sense of their experiences, but they got the chance to truly understand and reinvent themselves as individuals. As a result of this, they were also able to create a new partnership that was, by far, better than before.

They started their work as I am instructing you to start yours. In the same fashion, you need to operate from two basic premises. The first is understanding that the most counter-productive thing you can do is to try to force another person to change. This does not work because it invites resistance, sabotage, negativism, rebellion, and further distancing. The second premise entails focusing your energy on improving yourself. The first principle will liberate you to pursue the second, which is what really works.

When you try to change your spouse the implied message is that you believe there is something wrong with him. You are also implicitly blaming him for the problems in the marriage, while at the same time avoiding having to take responsibility for your own contributions to the marital dysfunction. This is particularly true if you have been criticizing, controlling, ridiculing, manipulating, or putting your partner down to get him to change.

Pressuring your mate to do what you want puts you in a parental position, and this is not healthy. It radically changes the nature of your relationship with him from a partnership into a parent-child dynamic. Your partner does not need a parent; he needs a partner.

If you have been doing this the smartest thing you can do to repair your marriage is to simply back off. One of the hallmarks of a loving, healthy marital relationship is granting an appropriate degree of freedom, while observing boundaries that protect the dignity of the individuals and the relationship between them.

Healthy boundaries allow partners the ability to be autonomous, responsible, motivated, genuine, and mature. As you back off from trying to fix your partner one of the first things you will notice is that you will begin to experience a sense of personal freedom yourself.

You will feel relieved once you give your partner space and time to be responsible for himself, and for his part in the marriage. Fire yourself from the position of being in charge of the relationship, and do not take responsibility for what does not belong to you.

What you can do instead is take initiative. Start working on becoming the kind of partner you want your husband to be. This is the most powerful way of influencing your partner by example. Your actions will give you credibility because your walk will match your talk. This type of change will also make him curious as to what is going on. He may start wondering about what you are doing because positive change is difficult to ignore.

Later on you may notice that he begins to pay more attention, and that he seems to like your new attitude and the behavior you display. Your consistency may cause him to start moving toward you, and to approach you more often.

Why do you suppose this is? It's because your positive change makes you come across as a more open, caring, and approachable partner. In this way his perspective and perception of you will improve, and he will naturally want to get closer to you.

In time you may notice that he starts doing some of the same things you are doing, as he feels safer in your presence. The general atmosphere of your relationship will continue to improve as your positive interactions reverse the damage of the disruptions from the past. Trust me, I am not kidding you about this, try it and you will see! I have seen it happen many times in my work with couples.

So I challenge you to be daring. You have two basic choices: Either you continue to repeat the same familiar and unhelpful patterns that are already at play in your marriage, or you start moving in the right direction by shifting your focus to the area where you can really use your energy and power to produce the changes you so desire.

PART 2

CHAPTER 4: A NEW BEGINNING

*"We cannot solve our problems with the same thinking
we used when we created them."*
Albert Einstein

The ancient poet Lucius Afranius once said, "The wise man will love; all others will desire." He and Albert Einstein were very smart men. Their words should tell you that if you want to solve your marital problems, you need to have a different approach in order to experience success.

As you embark in this creative journey to repair your marriage I also want you to realize that love is a transformative force in itself. When you give love, love will flow back to you. Love is action. Love is also a decision. Love is not magic or wishful thinking. It is not just a feeling, either. It is not enough to just desire love and positive change. It is not enough to just think about it. You must act on your desire to achieve the outcomes you want.

In order to create a new beginning for your relationship you want to always start on a positive note. This is very important because being in the midst of a troubled marriage has, more than likely, caused you to lose sight of "the good" in yourself, your partner, your marriage, and the life you share with him. To begin, I want you to complete the following exercise. If your partner also wants to do the exercise, that is even better, but he has to do it of his own volition and independently from you.

STEP 8 - EXERCISE FOR IDENTIFYING POSITIVE QUALITIES

1. Make a list of your positive qualities.

2. Make a list of your partner's positive qualities.

3. Make a list of the qualities of your marriage.

4. Share these lists with your spouse (if he is interested)

If you take time to create these lists, you will probably realize that you and your partner have valuable traits. These are what each of you bring to the table for creating a happy marriage. You will also become aware that these are the things that brought you and your husband together in the first place. The qualities of your marriage ought to make you acknowledge that the two of you do have the ability to create good things together. All these sets of qualities are "the funds" that you already have in the bank of your relationship.

In the days to come I want you to go out of your way to notice these, as well as other positive traits in yourself and in your partner. You can keep adding them to your list. Pay attention to your thoughts and feelings in this process. They are likely to improve your general outlook, and it may even make you feel more hopeful and positive. You may want to journal these experiences as well. This practice will allow you to nurture yourself by meeting your own needs, and by being an active agent in your process of self-improvement.

STEP 9 - EXERCISE FOR EVALUATING YOUR MARRIAGE

Next, go through the following list which I have created to evaluate the current state of your relationship. This will help you identify the strengths of your marriage, as well as the areas where growth is needed. Again, if your partner wants to complete this evaluation, he needs to do it on his own. This is important because his perspective and perception will, more than likely, be different from yours, at least in some areas.

Please be careful not to turn this exercise into a power struggle if you do this with your partner. Chances are you will disagree with him in some areas. Those areas are precisely the ones that will challenge you and him the most. Will this be difficult? Probably. Will it be impossible to work through? Absolutely not!

When people are motivated to work together and invest in the future of the relationship the sky is the limit. That has been my experience and observation over the years.

CHARACTERISTICS OF A HEALTHY MARRIAGE

Does your marriage have the following characteristics? To what degree? Assign a number on a scale of 1 to 10 (1 being the lowest, 10 being the highest):

☐   We trust each other.

☐   We respect each other.

☐   We know each other well.

☐   We admire and value each other.

☐   We are influential in each other's life.

☐   The boundaries in our relationship are clearly established and maintained by both of us.

☐   Our commitment to each other is consistent, clearly expressed, and demonstrated on a regular basis.

☐   Each of us is confident and secure in our own worth.

☐   We are willing to grow, take risks, and be vulnerable.

☐ We contribute to each other's happiness.

☐ We are able to take personal responsibility for our own behavior and happiness.

☐ We feel comfortable being emotionally and physically intimate.

☐ We meet each other's needs appropriately and in a balanced manner.

☐ We communicate openly and honestly on a regular basis.

☐ We are able to work through conflicts directly and resolve them in a fair and satisfactory manner.

☐ We are open to giving and receiving constructive feedback from each other.

☐ We are able to mutually give and receive from each other.

☐ We accept each other and refrain from trying to control, fix, or change each other.

☐ We are able to express assertively to each other our personal needs, feelings, and desires.

☐ We are able to let go of the need to be right when we disagree.

☐ When we make mistakes we are able to forgive ourselves and each other.

☐ We enhance each other's individuality, identity, and personal freedom.

☐ We support each other's personal growth.

☐ Each of us has some meaningful relationships, interests, and activities apart from the other.

☐ Each of us has personal space and we respect each other's privacy.

☐ We strike a balance between being close with each other and separate from each other.

☐ We make each other and our nuclear family the highest priority in our lives.

☐ We spend quality time as a couple and as a family regularly.

☐ We share duties and responsibilities in a fair and balanced fashion.

☐ _____

Hang on to the three lists of qualities you already created, as well as this list because you will need them to begin constructing a new guide or vision for your marriage. Creating a new paradigm for your marriage will be the map that guides you in the years to come so you and your partner can work together to succeed in the process of building the kind of marriage both of you want.

Imago Theory says that in order to build a happy partnership couples need to have a clear vision for what they want to see happen in the life of their marriage. Such a vision affords them purposeful direction. But I find it interesting that most couples take time to plan their wedding, buy a house, have children, grow their finances, build a career, plan for retirement, schedule vacations, and who knows what else.

Unfortunately, they do not do the same with their relationship. It is no wonder that later on they feel like their marriage is not what they envisioned when they first started. Years or decades into the marriage they feel like they are married to a stranger, an adversary, or a roommate with whom they have little in common.

Disappointment and disillusionment is common among these couples. These partners settle for lives of "quiet desperation", as Henry David Thoreau said. The ones that don't settle may try to escape through affairs, substance use, hobbies, work, or ultimately divorce.

Not having a clear plan for your marriage is like getting into sailboat together, having no idea as to where you want to go, and without a navigation map. The wind and the ocean currents of life will take you in whatever direction, and you may end up shipwrecked on some deserted island, having no idea as to where home is.

If you and your partner do not define what it is you want to see happen in the life of your marriage, who knows what might happen! And there is a really good chance that it won't be what you wanted in life. So, let's change that. Creating a new paradigm for your marriage will allow you and your partner to follow your own blueprint for success in the most important and impactful relationship of your life in the years to come.

You need to start defining what you want to see happen in your marriage, based on what is important to both of you. Once more, if your spouse wants to get involved in this process, that is great. If not, you can still do this on your own. If you do it together, remember that it should not be a competition of who gets to do what. The point is that both of you should get some of what you want.

For example, if financial security is important to the wife, then this ought to be included. If being able to use finances to support a hobby or passion which is important to the husband, then it needs to be included as well. This needs to always be done in a balanced way that is consistent with your individual and collective values, needs, and goals in life.

STEP 10 - EXERCISE FOR CREATING A NEW PARADIGM FOR YOUR MARRIAGE

Using the 3 lists of qualities, as well as the "Characteristics of a Healthy Marriage" evaluation, do the following:

1. Begin writing down the positive qualities that you and your spouse bring to the table. Then add the positive qualities of your marriage. These constitute "money in the bank", or the wealth you already possess together. They are also the things that need to be preserved, protected, and maintained in your relationship over the years.

2. Next, add the areas from the "Characteristics of Healthy Relationships" evaluation where both of you scored high (7 and above) Again, this is additional wealth in the bank of your marital relationship, which is "the good" that also needs to be preserved, protected and maintained to ensure the quality and strength of your marriage.

3. Finish the list by adding the areas where you scored 6 or less, as well as the areas where there is a significant disparity in your individual scores (if your spouse participated in this exercise)

These are the areas where there is room for growth and improvement.

Undoubtedly, these will represent a challenge for you and your partner. You will be required to stretch and grow individually and collectively. They will require your effort and commitment. Will this be easy? Perhaps not, but as I said before, if you really want it, you will intentionally invest your energy and resources to make good things happen.

This is the only way by which you can take your desire and turn it into reality. No amount of wishful thinking is going to create new realities in your life. I understand that this may seem like a daunting undertaking at first, but you have to start somewhere. This is no different than when you decided to attend school to become a teacher, doctor, lawyer, beautician, etc.

Imagine what would have happened if all you did was sit down to simply wish you would become a professional. I can guarantee that you would not have realized your dreams. No, you actually had to attend school for a number of years, put the hard work that goes into such an achievement, invest time, money and resources, pass many tests, and sacrifice yourself in various ways so you could enjoy the fruits of your labor.

Your marriage deserves the same kind of effort and investment.

4. Next, take time on a daily basis to enhance at least one of the positive aspects of yourself, your partner, and your marriage. This can take as little as a few minutes. Be intentional because you want to create positive new patterns in the relationship which will eventually become good habits.

5. Finally, work consistently on improving the challenging areas you identified, one at a time. Again, be intentional. Start with something reasonable for you. This will allow you to experience success in small ways, which will encourage and motivate you to continue moving forward.

    For example, you may want to start expressing yourself in ways that make it easier for your partner to listen to you, like being courteous toward him. This practice will definitely help improve the atmosphere of your marriage.

6. Place this new "map" for your marriage in an area of great visibility where you (and your partner) can see it regularly. It will serve as a visual reminder of what you need to be working on daily.

7. Take time to review this important document every 3 to 6 months to measure your progress. You can rate each of those areas every time you make a review to evaluate your efforts. At that time you can make any necessary changes as your relationship evolves over time. You may also want to add something or tweak something on the list. The sky is the limit.

   When you experience success, make sure to pat yourself on the back. If you see that your spouse is making progress, give him positive feedback to let him know that you are noticing his efforts, as this will increase his motivation to continue on the right track.

Note: If you and your spouse are able to raise the score of the challenging areas to an 8, you are doing really well. Use the 80/20 rule. If you are able to succeed in any of the areas 80% of the time, I would say that you are doing pretty well. Allow for some flexibility. Do not expect perfection.

BOUNDARIES IN MARRIAGE

This is an area of intimate relationships that merits special attention. Many relational problems stem from having poor boundaries, and marriages can be ruined because of that. I often encounter that couples believe that unity in marriage means that they have to give up their personal identity and individuality in order to build a cohesive partnership.

Such couples think that they need to sacrifice meaningful and important values and aspects of their own life on the altar of the marriage. At first they do it gladly because they are madly in love, which motivates them to abandon themselves in this manner. Eventually this catches up with them, however, as they begin to feel engulfed by the "oneness" of their marriage.

When I encounter this type of dynamic in a marriage, one or both partners are usually saying, "Honey, you and I are one, and I AM THE ONE!", as one of my Imago Therapy colleagues says. There is usually little or no room for personal space, differences, privacy, respect, individuality, self-agency, preferences, or freedom. In other words, they are joined at the hip like Siamese twins.

I heard a woman recently say on TV that she and her husband do EVERYTHING together, and she wondered if they were "nuts." My immediate thought was, "They need help." Couples like this one confuse love with possessing and controlling each other. They want to be involved in every aspect of the other's life, leaving little or no room to exercise their personhood.

These partners tend to expect compliance with their wishes, and when that doesn't happen they begin to experience rejection. But at some point in their enmeshed journey one or both partners begin to feel smothered. The struggle for power and control ensues, and much of the time these lovers resort to unhealthy tactics to get their way. Partners in these types of marriages see the other as "my other half", and instead of practicing self-control they are bent on controlling the other in overt or covert ways.

I can use the story of Max and Allie to illustrate this. They married in their late 20's after an 18 month dating and engagement period. Both were honest to admit that they did not know each other well before they married, but they thought they were a match made in heaven because they were both highly intelligent and sophisticated individuals. They also shared similar professional and life ambitions.

Both mates had dreams and expectations that they wanted to see fulfilled in their marriage, and these involved things that they wanted their "better half" to deliver. Honestly speaking, they entered marriage with an agenda in mind.

After the honeymoon stage of their marriage was over, they began to experience an intense power struggle that was exhausting for both of them. Allie, the more controlling and perfectionistic of the two, began to take over various aspects of Max's existence. At first he was happy to have a wife who was very adept at managing every aspect of his life, which he perceived as her taking good care of him.

Eventually, though, her "loving care" started to feel like a straight jacket that really cramped his style. He began to look for ways to get out of it. So he resisted complying with her demands and following her orders. When he did this, Allie resorted to crying because she felt rejected and victimized for trying to be good to him.

At first Max would comfort her and give in to her, but a few months later he felt manipulated by Allie's tears. He decided to ignore her whenever she cried. This tactic didn't work well, either. He came across as insensitive and arrogant. Allie would, in turn, react by becoming increasingly hostile, openly degrading Max by using shame, blame, and criticism. When this didn't make Max acquiesce Allie would shut down emotionally.

This pattern became a vicious cycle that in time made it increasingly more difficult for them to recover from the pain they caused each other. It also became the only way in which they interacted as a couple, as if negative attention was better than being completely ignored and feeling invisible altogether.

When both felt that all was lost they started treating each other with disdain and indifference, tacitly settling for living parallel lives that never converged anywhere.

They were emotionally divorced. At that point both were numb to the pain of their existence.

Through this agonizing process Max felt a tremendous mixture of emotions that ranged from anger to shame and guilt. He could not help feeling responsible for making Allie so terribly unhappy, but felt paralyzed to do anything constructive. He would frequently ask himself, "What happened to us?", "What did I do that was so wrong?, and "How did we get here?"

Allie had her own emotional suffering going on the entire time. She felt confused, angry, depressed, punished, and mistreated by Max. She was convinced that she had tried to be a loving, caring wife, only to be "slapped in the face", as she would say. She felt powerless to prevent the disintegration of her marriage, which was happening before her eyes. She eventually concluded that she had done everything she could to make it work, and gave up on it.

During a heated argument Allie confessed how she'd been feeling. Max retorted by doing the same. Both blamed each other for the marital problems, but neither ventured to offer solutions. Afterward, though, Allie escalated the conflict, fueled by the intense anger she felt. In a flash she thought that she could force a change by upping the ante.

All bets are off, she thought, so she began to spend more time shopping, going out with friends, and attending wild parties without even bothering to let Max know anything about her "private life." Flirting with other men, sometimes even in front of Max made her feel attractive, and she figured she could get his attention by making him feel jealous. She secretly also wanted to punish him for all the wrongs he'd committed against her, ruining her life.

Max shared at one of our sessions that at one point he had told Allie about feeling invisible and less important than the family dog. When this didn't seem to make an ounce of difference to her, Max further dug his heels in protest. That is when he made a conscious decision to ignore her crying, avoid her emotional tirades, and dismiss her hostility as if it didn't matter to him.

At the same time he decided that spending more time at work and exercising excessively would help him to avoid being at home with Allie. Of course, she noticed this, and it infuriated her, causing her to feel even more abandoned by Max.

To top it all off, he started criticizing her and making fun of her with his friends at work and at the gym, many of which knew Allie. When she found out about this she confronted him indignantly. On that day Max couldn't take it anymore, and in the middle of that heated argument he told his wife that he was done letting her control his life, and that he wanted out of the marriage. It was like a volcanic eruption and an earthquake all at once. "I don't care anymore", he said to her, as he felt that he had nothing more to lose at that point.

Allie was shocked. She felt an intense emotional blow that rattled her more than anything she had heard him say before. Max couldn't believe the words that came out of his mouth. Both realized at that point that they had wrongfully given themselves permission to behave poorly toward each other, based on the fact that their tactics were being tolerated on a daily basis. Neither realized how damaging their attitude and behavior had been until that very moment.

When they came to see me the one thing they agreed on was that both felt miserable, and wanted to find a way out. They were desperate. Needless to say, I didn't have to break the news to Max and Allie. They knew that their marriage was in serious trouble. Instead of divorcing immediately they decided to make a final attempt to repair their broken relationship.

This situation exemplifies many of the boundary problems commonly encountered in marriages today. Having appropriate limits in a marital relationship is essential to its success, as healthy boundaries have the following important functions:

1. **Definition:** Dr. Henry Cloud and Dr. John Townsend say that your boundaries define who you are as an individual, and that these need to

be communicated to others so they know who you are, and what you stand for. This is how you represent yourself honestly in your relationships. Being true to yourself, and letting others know what sets you apart allows you to be genuine. So it is extremely important and necessary that you communicate to your partner your values, goals, and beliefs.

Likewise, a couple that is heading for the altar needs to develop healthy boundaries for their marriage, based on their values and goals. These will help define and protect the relationship in a similar fashion. Some of these boundaries will be easily agreed upon, like being faithful to each other. Others may need to be negotiated to reach a consensus.

2. **Ownership and responsibility:** It is important for both marriage partners to be conscious of what is theirs to own and have domain over. You and your husband need to take personal responsibility for the things that fall within your own territory.

    Examples of this are being responsible for your physical health, your thoughts and emotions, your spiritual wellbeing, your work, your actions, as well as your contributions to the marital partnership.

3. **Protection:** Appropriate limits guard the things that are important to both partners in the marriage. They help protect the relationship from destructive outside influences. Examples of this are marital exclusivity, physical and emotional safety, confidentiality, making each other your highest priority, and investing the majority of your resources on the marriage.

4. **Right use of power:** Clear and appropriate limits allow each partner to use their power rightfully within the context of the marriage. The best example of this is the ability to exercise self-control instead of trying to control the other person. Flexible boundaries between marriage partners also need to allow both spouses to exercise a reasonable degree of influence on each other. In this fundamental manner the power in the relationship is properly shared.

5. **Facilitation:** Healthy boundaries in marriage help partners to interact, integrate, negotiate, invest, collaborate, create, resolve conflict, satisfy needs reasonably, as well as to develop the marital relationship toward maturity. The "us" in the marriage is prioritized, grown and nurtured in an atmosphere of safety, love, advocacy, and mutual respect.

    Good examples of this are finding common ground, communicating respectfully on a regular basis, resolving conflicts equitably and fairly, negotiating, making mutual concessions, and being able to grow closer through the cumulative effect of those experiences.

6. **Maturation:** Nothing else in life will require a husband and wife to grow and mature more than their marriage. I personally believe that marriage gives partners endless opportunities for becoming mature adults. As I have already suggested, your partner will need you to grow and stretch in areas of your personality that you need to develop and mature.

   Good examples of this are developing empathy, becoming inclusive of each other in making important joint decisions, controlling your emotions, as well as taking responsibility for your actions and the subsequent impact that these have on your mate and others involved.

In my work with couples I have found that when the topic of establishing and maintaining appropriate limits comes up, married couples typically think that it has to do with making each other change in some way, or in many ways.

By the time they come to see me, many of them have already been trying to do that for a long time, with poor results. So they say things like, "I've been trying to make her stop yelling", or "I can't tell you how tired I am of trying to make him do things the right way!"

These couples are very surprised when I tell them that, as Dr. Henry Cloud and Dr. John Townsend say, having appropriate boundaries is mainly about each individual developing the ability to exercise self-control. I add that it is also about becoming the kind of partner they desire the other to be.

The fact is that a great majority of people in troubled marriages limit themselves to blaming their spouse for the problems they are experiencing as a couple. This is a clear indication that there are issues in the boundary system of the relationship, which need to be addressed in order to improve it.

So if you can identify with this type of scenario, one of the radical shifts you need to make now is to take responsibility for your own contributions to the problems in the marriage. At the same time you need to start allowing your spouse to experience the logical and natural consequences of his or her choices, actions, and feelings.

If you are in the habit of rescuing your spouse from negative consequences, fire yourself from the job immediately. Your partner does not need a parent managing his life. He needs a partner who allows him to own his life, as well as his part in the marriage. I suggest that before you implement any changes you respectfully discuss with him what you are about to do, so he is not taken by surprise.

Let's take another look at the marriage between Allie and Max so we can identify the various boundary problems in their troubled relationship, which were present from the very beginning. When they first met they did a very typical thing, which is to rush things in the heat of romance. Since both of them deeply desired to keep the relationship going, they failed to take time to really get to know each other.

They did not consider the fact that it's impossible to truly love someone you really don't know. Both fell in love with the fantasy image they created about each other. They were exhilarated with the romantic feelings they experienced, as well as with the idea of getting married and having a fairy tale wedding.

By doing this they unfortunately failed to create a strong foundation for their marriage. They didn't take responsibility for their future, for how they invested themselves, for protecting their hearts, and for building a healthy relationship. Both confessed that they noticed red flags while dating, yet both chose to ignore them for fear of losing the relationship.

Because they were so determined to make things happen, both of them became "yes" people. They put their best foot forward to impress each other, and to keep the feelings going. Having the courage to say "no" to certain things was not in their repertoire, not wanting to upset each other or break the magic spell of their romance.

Neither Max nor Allie had the gumption to talk about their expectations, goals, personal values, or desires for the future of their relationship. Very early on they established a pattern of avoiding disagreements, conflicts, or being different from each other. Soon the "me and you" got completely lost in the "we", which both mistook for love.

This enmeshment caused both of them to lose their personal identity, lacking the courage to express their values, thoughts, desires, concerns or preferences openly. They only allowed themselves to express loving feelings, never discussing the ones that caused them distress.

In time their marriage became more of a parent-child relationship where Allie was the parental figure, and Max played the role of the child. She took care of him, and he let her. The more she did, the less he had to worry about. As is typical of this type of dynamic, he eventually resented her for "controlling" him, then rebelled in a desperate attempt to regain his autonomy.

These two did not understand that as marriage partners they were responsible to each other, not for each other.

Neither one took responsibility for their personal thoughts, feelings, desires, or behavior along their painful path. Naturally, all they did was blame each other for their unhappiness.

As time went along instead of growing and maturing in the marriage this couple increasingly regressed to earlier stages of development. Both partners began to act out in very spiteful ways toward each other, destroying their marriage. They disrespected each other and broke the trust by exiting the relationship through rather inappropriate behaviors. They also disregarded each other's needs, wounded each other deeply, and became very unlovable individuals themselves.

Doctors Henry Cloud and John Townsend have written excellent books on boundaries, and I recommend that you take the time to learn from their wisdom if this is a particularly troublesome area of your marriage. For the purposes of this book, I want to address the general aspect of enmeshment or disconnection in marital relationships, as this is a very common boundary problem, and a source of conflict between marriage partners.

ENMESHMENT OR DISCONNECTION

Let me start by describing what a healthy interpersonal connection looks like. As I said before, when a couple shares a healthy bond of connection there are appropriate boundaries that define each partner within the context of the marriage. Both partners are complete individuals in their own right, not halves of a whole.

These individuals are inter-connected, interact with each other, and feel comfortable being separate from each other when appropriate. There's also fluidity in their process of engaging each other and disengaging from each other. When there is a healthy bond or attachment between marriage partners there is a balance between engagement and disengagement.

Healthy partners are inter-dependent and receptive to each other, not overly dependent on each other. Both partners view each other as separate individuals who have domain over themselves, yet allow their partner to influence them in various ways. They value each other's opinions, consider each other's needs, respect each other's rights, and honor each other's wishes. Both partners embrace similarities they share, as well as differences between them.

These partners understand that they can be close at times, and that they can retreat to their own corner of the world when necessary. They embrace all aspects of their personalities. They are able to tolerate differences of opinion and disagreements, and are curious about each other's perspectives and realities.

They are able to empathize with each other, and they

welcome emotional expression. They make joint and independent decisions when appropriate, while taking into consideration that their personal decisions affect the other. Both partners are invested in meeting each other's needs in a balanced manner, are supportive of each other, and work together to solve conflicts.

When one or both partners lack well defined personal boundaries, on the other hand, there is a tendency for partners to be enmeshed or fused with each other. Neither partner knows where one ends and where the other begins. Enmeshed partners are defined by each other and by the relationship, rather than by their own values, preferences, desires, or personal style.

These marriages are marked by codependence. There may be immaturity, insufficient autonomy, lack of individuality and personal freedom, as well as poor self identity. Both partners are excessively involved in each other's existence, as if their own life is being lived through the other.

This was the case of Myrna and Carter. They were truly joined at the hip. He could not even order a meal independently at a restaurant. He had to ask her what she planned to order so he could order the same dish. Neither allowed the other to be different in any way, or have a basic degree of separateness.

Conflict arose every time differences came up between

them because they perceived them as a threat to their closeness. Needless to say, they argued about these issues on a daily basis.

This dyad prided themselves in being able to finish each other's sentences, which in reality was more like interrupting each other and expressing their own ideas as the other's. As I got to know them better I learned that both partners grew up in very enmeshed families that functioned as a whole, not allowing its members individual differentiation. I call these families "caterpillar families" because all the members "move" together. They are controlled and defined by their sameness, as well as by the need to spend a lot of time together.

Growing up in the culture of such families, Carter and Myrna were intrusive and disrespectful, and they blamed each other for violations that they themselves were guilty of. Lots of work had to go into helping these two in becoming well defined individuals who could be close and separate at the same time.

Emotionally disconnected couples, on the other hand, are pretty much the opposite of enmeshed couples. These partners are distant, overly self-sufficient, and self-absorbed. They have difficulty being vulnerable with each other and are fearful of emotional intimacy. Their disengagement can be visible, as they often live parallel lives that don't intersect anywhere.

In this type of relationship one or both partners are

pretty unaware of what the other is going through, and their interactions are limited to emotionless exchanges. They usually find it safe to limit their interactions to sharing information in an impersonal way, or go about their business while ignoring each other. They don't talk about their feelings, problems, desires, aspirations, or dreams. This kind of relational disengagement is very troublesome because there's usually little or no emotional energy to invest in trying to re-invent the relationship.

It is also true that some couples are comprised of one enmeshed individual and a disconnected other. This is a very interesting paradigm. The enmeshed partner is the over-functioning one, and the disengaged partner is the under-functioning one. The over-functioning partner usually plays the role of a parent or authority figure. The under-functioning one tipically plays the role of the child or subordinate.

I suggest that you take some time to explore and reflect on this important topic. The following exercise can help.

STEP 11 - EXERCISE FOR IDENTIFYING ENMESHMENT OR DISCONNECTION IN MARRIAGE

The list that follows contains an exhaustive compilation of behaviors that indicate relational enmeshment or disconnection in a marriage. If what I've discussed in this regard rings a bell for you, review this list primarily with you in mind. Those are the ones that you will need to work on to improve the dynamics in your marriage.

Addictions
   (Alcohol, drugs, prescription drugs, porn, gambling, phone, computer, TV, video games, sex, food, shopping, spending, or friends)
Affairs (sexual/emotional/casual)
Assuming
Attacking (verbally/physically)
Avoiding
Being angry/hostile
Being authoritative/authoritarian (parenting role)
Being bossy
Being chronically late
Being controlling
Being cynical
Being depressed (and unwilling to get help)
Being dishonest (lying/withholding information)
Being distrustful/suspicious
Being hard to please
Being immature
Being impatient
Being inconsiderate
Being insensitive
Being irresponsible
Being irritable/touchy/uptight/tense
Being judgmental
Being negative/pessimistic
Being offensive/abusive
Being overly dependent/needy/clingy
Being overly independent
Being passive/aggressive
Being perfectionistic

Being a pleaser
Being preoccupied
Being pushy
Being resentful
Being rigid/stubborn
Being rude
Being sarcastic
Being self-absorbed/selfish
Being uncaring
Being uncooperative
Being unreliable
Being unsupportive
Believing you're right all the time
Blaming
Breaking agreements/promises
Coercing
Condemning
Criticizing
Disengaging
Disrespecting boundaries
Domineering
Eating/overeating
Embarrassing/shaming/ridiculing
Fault finding/nitpicking
Forgetting
Going silent/keeping silent
Ignoring
Interrupting
Isolating
Keeping secrets
Mindreading
Nagging
Name calling

Neglecting
Over-focusing on children/friends/family/hobby/looks
Over-functioning (parental role)
Overworking
Procrastinating
Punishing
Sabotaging
Shutting down
Taking on too much responsibility
Threatening (explicitly or implicitly)
Under-functioning (child-like role)
Withdrawing
Withholding affection/sex
Withholding your opinion/emotions

1. Now take some time to identify the behaviors that you engage in from the above list. Circle them or mark them in some way.

2. When you are finished, I want you to pick one to work on. Next, come up with three alternative, more appropriate and adaptive behaviors that can replace it.

   For example, if you are in the habit of blaming your partner, you can start taking responsibility for your own contribution to the problems in the marriage. If your tendency is to yell at your spouse, you would want to practice speaking to him in a respectful tone of voice on a regular basis.

3. In a few weeks you can pick another behavior

from the list and start working on improving it consistently.

4. Maintain the behaviors that you have been able to modify.

5. You can journal about your process of changing and becoming the best partner you can be.

6. You may want to get feedback from your partner regarding your progress. This will provide a sense of accountability for you.

CHAPTER 5: CREATING A POSITIVE SHIFT

"Appreciation can make a day, even change a life. Your willingness to put it into words is all that is necessary."
Margaret Cousins

As we discussed before, one of the easiest ways for you to start creating love, passion, meaning, happiness, and satisfaction in your marital relationship is to start paying attention to the positive aspects of your partner. Noticing the positive traits, good intentions, caring gestures, and other demonstrations of love by your mate will permanently shift your focus from the negative to the positive. I am sure that you have already noticed this if you started applying the exercises in the previous chapters.

This concept is of great importance because when marriage partners are dissatisfied with each other they tend to focus on the negative in an attempt to fix it. This may be particularly true if you have the tendency to over-function in your marriage. If this is the case, by now you probably have already gone from trying to fix your marriage to trying to fix your partner.

This, as I said several times before, will have adverse repercussions for you. One of the main reasons why such misguided attempts fail is because when you consistently focus on the negative, eventually this negative focus becomes the only lens through which you view the other person. This is like putting on a pair of dark glasses that filter out all "the good" in your mate.

This creates a shift toward the negative. You may not have even realized when this started happening, but your perception of him has changed. As a matter of fact, this negative bias will cause your brain to start looking for evidence that confirms the negative mindset you have developed about your partner. It's no wonder that so many husbands and wives in distressed marriages believe that their spouse has changed. Both partners may feel like they are under a microscope where only their faults are noticed day in and day out.

If your partner knows that he only gets negative attention from you when he does something that displeases you, he won't want your attention. If he only gets nagged or criticized by you, he will turn his attention to other things and other people. He will gradually distance from you, eventually disconnecting from you in order to avoid emotional pain and hassles. This instinct for self-preservation makes sense, right? No one likes to get close to someone with whom they have an abundance of negative experiences.

He may start overworking, spending more time on his personal interests, socializing without you, staying out late, etc. In other words, he will disengage in order to survive the situation. Generally speaking, when wives experience rejection and neglect from their husbands, they typically turn to over-focusing on their children, friends, shopping, over-eating, etc. They may also get anxious and depressed.

What is most interesting is that when such dynamics are at play, unconsciously both partners start behaving in a manner that actually induces the other to act in prescribed ways that enact their own internal drama. Their personal conflict and narrative are related to experiences they each had in their relationship with their parents while they were growing up. To say it succinctly, this is the "unfinished business" from the past which gets re-created in their marriage.

Let me illustrate this complex principle with the story of a couple in their 40's named Larry and Marlene. Larry grew up in poverty with a very critical single mother who, unless he was in some kind of trouble, she'd pay little attention to him. When Larry did something that displeased his mother, she'd yell at him and send him to his room for long periods of time.

During each of her tirades she would blame him for her personal misery and for their poverty because she believed that her life would be much better, had Larry never been born. And she told him as much on a regular basis. So Larry grew up feeling like a mistake and learned to worry about money from a very early age. He remembered vowing to make lots of money when he grew up, as he came to believe that money was the most important thing in life, and what defined his worth.

Marlene, on the other hand, grew up with her widowed father and his various girlfriends. Her father traveled quite a bit and left her to the care of these women who were rather indifferent toward her. She recalled feeling like she didn't matter to anyone. Marlene escaped her feelings of worthlessness, loneliness, and insignificance by frequently rehearsing fantasies of marrying a man who'd rescue her and make her happy, just like the handsome, rich princes from the fairy tale stories she knew so well.

When Marlene met Larry she was sure that he was her prince. Their romance was intense and their wedding was all that she hoped for. Larry also believed that Marlene was his soul mate. He had always wanted to marry someone who truly needed him and would be impressed by his many accomplishments. He wanted to make her happy.

About a year into their married life things began to fall apart. Larry immersed himself in his work and Marlene in her social life. Early in the marriage he assumed that since Marlene enjoyed the affluent lifestyle he provided, all was well at the ranch. Marlene would not dare communicate with him about her feelings of loneliness because she feared he'd leave her.

The marriage was in a state of crisis by the time they sought my assistance. Larry was aware that his number one priority was his career and earning a very good income. After all, this was his way of taking good care of his wife and kids. But how would he know about her intense loneliness since they did not recall ever having truly intimate conversations where they discussed such things? He didn't even notice what was going on right in front of him.

With such a chasm between them, Marlene increasingly became very critical of Larry over their five year marriage. In her opinion, Larry was nothing but a workaholic who only cared about money. She also felt like a single mother because Larry did not participate in parenting their children.

She was anxious and depressed because, needless to say, she felt that Larry neglected and rejected her and their children. In time this led her to focus on all the negative things she saw in her husband. She no longer appreciated the fact that he was very committed to providing for her and the family. Marlene's critical attitude and hurtful complaints were meant to put pressure on Larry to pay attention to her and the children.

The more Larry worked and failed to meet Marlene's unmet emotional needs, the more Marlene complained and criticized. Larry would then distance from her, as he felt very uncomfortable dealing with conflict in the marriage, and would simply avoid it by going to work.

Marlene in turn perceived his distancing as indifference

and abandonment, much like what she had experienced with her father during her childhood and adolescence. Larry, on the other hand, would frequently regret marrying someone who, like his mother, saw him as a huge mistake and emasculated him with her daily criticism and negativity. Marlene would tell herself that Larry was just a "cold fish" who had simply turned out to be a huge disappointment to her. He was nothing like the prince she thought she married.

Can you see how these troublesome dynamics can destroy a marriage? I recommend that you take some time to think about your own family history and the history of your marriage so you can discern how this may relate to you and your mate. Developing insight in this area will help you understand what is going on in your relationship. It is quite possible that the emotional wounds each of your brought into the marriage need to be healed.

Generating a positive shift to begin healing your marital relationship is of paramount importance. If you and your spouse fail to notice, acknowledge, and value the good in each other, you will distance or completely disconnect emotionally. You will also feel taken for granted. Your emotional wounds will continue to compound, never having a chance to heal.

I've had many husbands and wives tell me that they feel invisible in their distressed marriage. Some husbands have expressed feeling like they are only a paycheck. Some wives say that they feel like they are only the maid or a sexual object. I think that this is rather sad.

You know, there will always be some other woman out there who notices your husband's good qualities and tells him how much she admires him. Or there may be some unscrupulous man somewhere who tells your wife that she is beautiful and lovable. Many extra-marital affairs start this way. That other woman is telling your husband what he needs to hear from you. That slick guy may just convince your wife to become his lover and destroy your marriage and family in the process.

On a lighter note, I chuckle when I remember Tanya and Art, a couple who struggled with chronic marital troubles. Whenever she'd say to him, "we need to talk", he'd respond by saying, "Fine, cut to the chase and just tell me what I did wrong." I am sure you don't think this is very funny if that is the norm in your interactions with your husband.

So the way to continue turning the tide is to keep taking time to focus on the positive. Do you remember noticing the good in your spouse at the beginning of your relationship? I bet you noticed plenty. That is why you liked him and were attracted to him in the first place.

But noticing is not enough because your partner cannot read your mind. One of the worst assumptions you can make is that he can read your mind. I cannot tell you how many partners I have heard say, "Oh, but he knows how I feel about him, why do I have to keep saying those things?", or "I have already told her what I like about her, do I have to keep repeating myself?"

Well, I am here to tell you that you do need to keep expressing these things, and to do it daily. And I mean daily. This practice is food for the soul because human beings need to feel like they matter. They like to be visible, important, and worthy of attention. They need to know that they are valuable in the eyes of their partner, and to be viewed in a positive light.

Feeling invisible is very damaging for the human psyche. This is why in many relationships the opposite of love is not hatred, it is indifference. Indifference denies the importance of the individual and results in feelings of worthlessness, as if they do not matter to others. I have had some partners tell me that even the dog gets more loving attention from their mate than they do. And that is an incredibly sad reality in some cases.

You have probably experienced emotional pain related to being ignored, unimportant, unappreciated, taken for granted, or unloved by people who matter to you. You don't want to inflict the same kind of suffering on your mate. Take initiative and start to turn things around if you have already hurt your partner in this way.

The following exercise is designed to help you learn how

to express to your partner what you appreciate or admire in him. I usually tell couples that doing this simple exercise daily is like making small deposits in the bank of their relationship on a regular basis.

STEP 12 - EXERCISE FOR EXPRESSING APPRECIATION, ADMIRATION, OR AFFIRMATION

Once a day, take a moment (it takes one minute or less) to express to your partner in one or two short sentences one thing you appreciate or admire in him. It can be about a quality he has, a loving gesture, or a simple helpful act on his part. Or it could be something hugely significant for you. Be specific and express it in positive terms.

I have included some examples of appreciations for you to get the gist of it.

- Today I appreciate that you brought me a cup of coffee. That really helped me to get to work on time.

- I so admire that you are diligent in your work. You are a good provider, and your effort means a lot to me.

- I admire the fact that you are compassionate toward others and willing to help them. That has always attracted me to you.

- Thank you for giving me feedback about our son's problems. It gave me a new perspective on it.

- Your sense of humor at the party last night was excellent. I enjoyed having fun with you.

If your spouse wants to join you in this exercise, that is even better. One day you initiate the exercise, and he follows by doing the same after you. The next day he goes first, and you go second. You can continue the process by taking turns initiating the exercise each day.

If you and your mate decide to do this exercise together it is very important that both of you refrain from reminding, nagging, criticizing, or complaining if one of you forgets to initiate the exercise when it's their turn to start it. Neither one of you needs a parent. Both of you need a mature partner who takes responsibility for making positive contributions to the space of your relationship.

This is one of the ways in which the two of you can maintain balance in the process of creating a healthy relationship. My experience with this exercise is that it is very effective for improving the general atmosphere of a marriage.

If you practice it consistently it will become a great habit that will maintain the positive focus in your partnership.

Couples usually like it so much that they start doing it more than once a day. That makes sense, right? People like to be noticed in a positive way that makes them feel valued by their partner.

As you become more comfortable with this exercise, you may want to expand it by expressing to your partner why such things are important to you, how his contributions or efforts benefit you, how this helps you heal and grow, or what is meaningful for you about it. Make sure that you do not use this exercise to express veiled criticisms, to put down your partner, or to be sarcastic or insulting.

Here are some examples of what that would sound like:

- Thanks for being quiet at dinner last night. It finally gave others a chance to say something.

- I'm glad you finally started a diet. If you lose weight I may want to have sex with you.

- I appreciate that you have stopped arguing with me about stupid things, don't go there again!

- I admire that you are not as bitchy and nagging as you used to be.

- It makes me happy that you got a job. I am tired of having to take care of you all these years.

CHAPTER 6: MAINTAINING YOUR CONNECTION

"The most important reason for dating your spouse is to help both of you feel loved, valued, and cared for."
Travis N. Turner

As the above quote indicates, spending quality time as a couple is extremely important for nurturing each other and your marital relationship. Think back to the early stages of your dating, engagement, and marriage. Do you recall both of you making time to spend with each other? Wasn't it fun to escape, even for a little while to do something you enjoyed together? I bet thinking about it makes you smile as you reminisce.

When couples don't take time to have fun together boredom sets in, and those feelings of longing for each other tend to go by the wayside. After a while you and your partner feel like you are roommates instead of lovers. Life as a couple becomes a boring and hectic routine where only the realities and responsibilities of daily existence are attended to.

It is very easy for couples to get into a rut that makes their marriage seem more like a life sentence than a loving partnership. I have heard that the difference between a rut and a grave is just the dimensions. This is especially true when it comes to long-term relationships.

Some couples so neglect each other over the years that

they get to the point where they can't even remember the happy times as they look back at their life together. This is a sign of real trouble in any marriage.

You may have watched the routine that brilliant comedian and ventriloquist Jeff Dunham does with his puppet Walter, who says that marriage is like a Slurpee: you take the first two sips, and it tastes great…and you tell yourself that it's good…you're glad you got married. As you keep drinking it, though, all you get is a brain freeze, making you go, ARGH!!! For many marriages this is sad, but true.

Troubled couples face tough realities in their life together, and this is regrettable. I usually ask these spouses, "Do you think you would have gotten married if you spent as little time with each other when you started dating, as you do now?" The answer is always a resounding "No!!" I get the same answer when I ask them, "Would you have married if you thought in the beginning of your courtship that your marriage would be so disappointing?"

Ask yourself these same questions. I am quite sure that your marriage did not start out this way. What happened is that both of you neglected your relationship and allowed it to go sour, or to perish altogether. You simply dropped the ball and stopped playing. It is no wonder that you don't feel emotionally connected to each other.

Imagine what would happen if you drained your bank account of all its funds and neglected making any deposits to replenish it. One day you show up at your bank to withdraw one million dollars. If you and your partner were bold enough to try this, I am sure that the teller would look at you kind of funny at first. Then she would quickly bring you back to reality by telling you that you have no funds in your account whatsoever. Think of your marriage along the same lines. There will be no wealth to enjoy if you fail to invest in it.

So it seems very logical that if you want to be close to your spouse, you need to make important improvements to make this happen. You and your partner need to make each other the number one priority in each other's life. No excuses. The truth is that people invest time, effort, and money on the people and things that are truly important to them.

Dating your spouse does not have to be expensive or take oodles of time. At a minimum, you and your mate need to be spending 2 hours of uninterrupted quality time with each other on a weekly basis, away from the children, and away from distractions that normally grab your attention (like the phone, the computer, television, video games, friends, hobbies, etc.)

If you think this is a lot to ask of you, think again. According to the A.C. Nielsen Co., the average American watches more than 4 hours of TV each day. Additionally, an eMarketer study in July 2013 showed that the average adult spends about 5 hours a day on their digital devices. So spending 2 hours a week giving each other undivided attention is minor compared to that.

It is also unfortunate to see that many couples shift all their energy, time, effort, and attention to caring for their children, and they stop being a couple altogether. You simply cannot have a balanced life and a strong family without being a strong couple first. Some couples even use their children as a safety buffer or wedge between them to avoid getting close. Granted, it is important and necessary to be good parents, but never at the expense of the marriage.

What these couples fail to realize is that having a happy and healthy marriage is the most important thing they can do for their children. Marriage partners need to remember that one day the children will leave, and the two of them will be facing each other once more. If you fail to nurture the relationship with your partner you will be spending the latter part of your life with a stranger.

So let's look at what happens in the human brain when couples keep doing the same things day in and day out, falling into routines or ruts that are boring and lifeless. With the lack of external stimuli the production of neurotransmitters involved with pleasure and novelty drops, and it remains low unless it gets regular doses of meaningful interaction and activities.

So your brain needs to be regularly stimulated by new and pleasurable experiences with your mate in order to create the right chemistry between the two of you. When spouses spend time having fun with each other, they feel more connected and satisfied. Isn't being together the main reason why you and your spouse got married in the first place?

The next exercise is designed to help you start making your brain (and his) do what it is supposed to do while spending quality time together.

STEP 13 - EXERCISE FOR CREATING NOVELTY IN YOUR MARRIAGE

I encourage you (and your partner) to take some time to create a list of fun activities you could do together. Be creative and think outside the box; it will be fun. Just remember, this is not a competition, it needs to be a joint effort. You can do it in one of two ways:

1. Each of you can make a list of what you would personally enjoy doing, and afterward share the lists with each other. As you go about your dating you can alternate picking one activity from each list, scheduling it, and then doing it.

   It is also a good idea for each of you to take turns making the necessary arrangements, such as planning the activity, getting a babysitter, making a reservation, finding out information, getting a map, buying tickets, etc. Make sure you follow through with it. And unless an emergency comes up, your time together needs to be of the highest priority.

2. The other approach you can try is for the two of you to sit together and brainstorm ideas for your dates. Take an hour or two to create a combined list of your preferences. Be adventurous. After you have completed the list you can start executing it by taking one activity at a time and going through the planning process described above. You can plan together or take turns. Then simply go do it.

   Talk about the experience with your mate afterward. You may want to mark the activities you enjoyed the most with an asterisk, as you and your partner may want to repeat them later on. Consider the possibility of turning any one of those activities into a shared hobby you can enjoy together.

3. You may also want to include a few surprises here and there, provided your partner does not mind them (some people do) Tell your partner you have a pleasant surprise for him, tell him the date and time when he needs to be ready, and what the appropriate attire is for the activity.

You plan the whole thing, keeping in mind that the activity you choose is to please your spouse, not yourself.

For example, I remember that several years ago I realized that my husband always made plans for our Valentine's Day celebration. So, it occurred to me that it would be good for me to take the initiative with that once in a while. So I did exactly what I'm instructing you to do.

I planned the activity down to the smallest detail, and on top of it I decided to spice things up by blindfolding him just prior to our little adventure (it makes us smile every time we reminisce about it...we just loved it!) Of course, I put him in the car blindfolded and drove him to the event.

He simply could not believe that I would do such a thing, but laughed the whole way to our destination. He even said to me several times, "What if the neighbors or the police see us...me, blindfolded and all... they will think you are kidnapping me!" "So what, you are my husband, and you came willingly...I will tell them the truth", I responded as we laughed heartily.

I'd venture to say that this was one of our most memorable Valentine's celebrations ever! Such great memories are for a lifetime. They are gifts that keep on giving because of the treasured memories, the love and the laughter.

You too can be creative and come up with great ideas for having a good time together. If money is an object, there are a lot of free or low cost activities you can do. Here's a short list of them:

- Put the children in bed half an hour early on a Friday evening and have a picnic in the privacy of your bedroom. Put a STOP sign on the door so they do not interrupt. This works like a charm because children usually like their parents being romantic with each other.

- Go for a walk at a place that you have never been to before, like a park or a lake.

- Visit a library or bookstore where you can look through books that you are interested in.

- Do a scavenger hunt in your home or yard using romantic clues.

- Play a board game and the winner gets a foot or back massage.

- Cook a new meal together and enjoy it by candlelight with quiet music in the background. Reminisce about the good times you've had together.

- Have a sharing time where you tell each other things about your childhood, family, friends, adolescence, vacations, etc. that you have never mentioned before.

- Visit places you frequented when you started dating. Talk about those experiences.

- Take time to look at your wedding pictures or video and share feelings about that day.

- Wake up early and go to the beach to watch the sunrise together.

- Stay up late and go outside to look at the stars.

- Pick one that can become your own star and remind you of each other. Give it a name that symbolizes the love you share.

- Read a book together taking turns reading the chapters. Share ideas and feelings that came up for you at the end of each chapter.

- Share your spiritual beliefs and pray together.

- Take a bubble bath by candlelight with soft music in the background.

- Spend time lying next to each other sharing your

dreams, touching, caressing, or giving each other a massage.

- Go for a drive or bike ride. Do not talk about problems. Talk about the things that attracted you to each other when you first met.

- Tell your spouse your best dream or desire for his life. Talk about how the two of you could work together to make that happen. Talk about your own best dream and highest desire in life, and how you can work together to make that happen.

- Put one dollar (each) in a jar each day, and when it's full go out somewhere fun, just the two of you.

Years ago I helped a man who had very limited financial resources, but really wanted to convey his love for his wife on her birthday. He mentioned that she had shown him a picture of a beautifully decorated bathroom which she had seen in a magazine, and he wished that he could give her that on her birthday.

I suggested that he be creative and try to reproduce the ambiance in their humble bathroom, to the best of his ability. After following my suggestion he reported that his wife was brought to tears when he showed her his version of that beautiful bathroom. He told me that she could not believe that he'd go to such effort to show her his love. He spent less than $ 5.00 making this happen.

As you can see, there are many options for conveying your love while engaging your partner in meaningful ways. Make a habit of coming up with new ideas, and repeat the ones you both enjoyed. Be creative in bringing novelty to your partnership, and at the same time create rituals that can make your marriage unique, intimate, and interesting.

CHAPTER 7: PUTTING THE HORSE BEFORE THE CART

"Actions speak louder than words."   American Idiom

Love is much more than a feeling. Love is a verb. It's a decision that needs to be demonstrated through actions. It is impossible for a couple to be emotionally connected without genuinely demonstrating the love they profess for each other. Unfortunately, after the romantic stage of the relationship, many partners slowly stop acting in ways that communicate their love for their mate.

Usually this happens as the passionate feelings begin to subside, and conflicts start rearing their ugly head. I can assure you that this is the normal progression of committed relationships. So I will venture to guess that this has already happened to you. Before you even realized it, the magic was gone, and you started wondering how that happened. And, like I said before, there is a really good chance that you and your partner took for granted that your love would last forever without having to work for it.

This is like buying a nice tree, throwing it into a dark corner of your garage, and forgetting all about it. You failed to plant it in a nice sunny spot somewhere in the yard. You forgot to water it, fertilize it, apply insecticide, or prune the dead branches.

You wrongly assumed that it would take care of itself, and that it would just keep growing.   You expected it to produce delicious fruit on a regular basis, and for a lifetime. You probably also expected the tree to look beautiful, and to provide shade for you and your family.

What a big surprise, indeed, when you went looking for the fruit on the tree, only to realize that not only had the tree failed to produce fruit, but that it was actually dying. It is the same way in marriage. You cannot expect to reap the benefits of your relationship when you neglect it or ignore it day in and day out.

If you completed the exercises in the previous chapters you have already created considerable momentum in the process of generating positive changes in your marriage. If you want to continue moving forward you must invest additional energy into reinventing your relationship.

Hopefully your partner has been responsive to your efforts and has participated in this important journey. If that is the case, without even realizing it both of you have helped create synergy in your partnership. Synergy in marriage is a process where the combined effect of both partners' efforts is greater than the sum of its parts. In other words, 1+1= 3.

Small positive contributions from each of you to the sacred space of your relationship have an exponential effect that will keep your marriage alive and strong. Of course, if your partner is not doing his part, you can still continue to do yours and see what happens. Trust me, in the end it will be better than doing nothing.

Of course, this does not mean that you have to be the only one who makes all the effort from now until the end of time. It does mean, however, that if you do your part long enough and he doesn't, this is valuable information that will help you ascertain whether your marriage is viable anymore. You can make important decisions based on this information.

For now let's continue to focus on how you can keep doing your part. Many couples in troubled marriages have told me that they would start acting more lovingly when the good feelings return, especially when their partner "starts acting nicer." That is nonsense!

When I hear this I usually respond by telling them that they need to put the horse before the cart, and not the other way around. If you don't continue to create momentum, the cart is going to stay right where it is. No amount of wishful thinking is going to make it move even an inch.

The truth is, the positive feelings will start to come back AFTER you engage in intentional, deliberate, loving actions and attitudes. Imagine for a moment what would happen if you were to expect getting paid without showing up at work, or actually performing your duties.

Logically, you would not get a dime, and you would be

sadly disappointed. Not only that, but when you show up to collect you would be fired on the spot.

I want you to realize something very important, and that is that you and your mate already know how to demonstrate your love for each other because you did it in the beginning of the relationship. This means that both of you have the ability to be loving, caring partners. You just need to start exercising this ability once more.

So let's go down memory lane for a moment. Do you remember how you and your beloved used to perform loving and caring actions when you started dating? Do you recall how open and positive your attitude was toward each other? I am sure you can, and I can tell you that you can rekindle the love and passion in your marriage, and possibly make your marriage the best that it can be.

If you start bringing all the wonderful things you were able to do in the past into the present, you will continue to transform your relationship. The loving feelings will flow once more, and you will be able to fall in love all over again. I can tell you without a doubt, that this is what both of you are yearning for. So, it's time you go about making the horse pull the cart.

The next step in this process involves an exercise which is designed to do exactly that. Again, it will be fantastic if your partner wants to join you in a parallel fashion. If he doesn't, you can still do this unilaterally. The only thing you need him to do would be to complete the form below for you to use as a guide for loving him in the way that he wants to be loved by you.

STEP 14 - EXERCISE FOR CREATING LOVING ACTIONS

Each partner creates a list of specific behaviors that the other partner can do which are meaningful, nurturing, loving, caring, and self-esteem enhancing for them. Make sure to be positive and specific. Include the frequency in which you would like to see these behaviors occur (e.g. once a week, once a day, etc.) Do not list frustrations. List at least three behaviors in each section.

Tips For Creating Your Loving Actions List

- **Be clear** – Describe in simple terms what you want ("I want us to hold hands when we go out...")

- **Be specific** – Focus on clearly defined actions you desire from your partner ("When you come home, and before you greet the children, I would like to have a kiss and a hug...")

- **Be positive** – Describe what you want rather than what you don't want ("I need you to express appreciation when I cook a good meal for us..." Instead of "I want you to stop criticizing...")

Let's get started:

1. Each partner needs to complete a list of the actions, behaviors, words, or symbolic things that the other did in the past, which made you feel special, loved, cared for, appreciated, important, or nurtured. Be very specific and concrete as you focus on actions that your partner can start performing again to convey love to you.

Example: What you did in the past that made me feel loved, and would like to see happen again is...

    A.

    B.

    C.

    D.

    E.

    F.

2. List specific things that your partner is doing presently, which communicate love, caring, or concern to you.

Example: What you are currently doing, which makes me feel cared for, special, and important is when you...

    A.

    B.

C.

D.

E.

F.

3. List any caring, loving actions that you have always wanted, needed, imagined, or desired from your partner, which you have never asked for.

Example: I would feel cherished, excited, or thrilled if you would...

A.

B.

C.

D.

E.

F.

Listed below are examples of loving actions:

- Once a month I would like you to put in my briefcase, on my pillow, or my mirror a love note telling me a quality that you like in me.

- On Saturday or Sunday morning I would like you to bring me a cup of coffee or glass of juice and the newspaper.

- I used to love it when you called me once a day to ask me how my day is going.

- It would thrill me if you started using a pet name or term of endearment for me which has a special meaning for us.

- Ask me out for a date once a month/week/etc.

- Surprise me twice a year by arranging a babysitter and taking me for an overnight stay at my favorite...

- Once a day you offer to help me with...

- Give me an affirmation or compliment about my role as a mother when you see me being a good parent to our children.

- Ask my opinion on something that is important to you once a week/month/etc.

- It would please me if you washed and waxed my car once a month.

- I'd like you to hold me in bed for 15 to30 minutes once a month and let me talk about my dreams, hopes, and desires for our future together.

- Let me initiate sex once a....

- Give me a short appreciation about something I did or said before we go to bed at night.

- Bring me a rose or flowers on a special occasion at least once a year.

- Tell your parents or friends in my presence one thing you like or appreciate about me once a month.

- Touch me gently and lovingly once a day.

- Whisper sweet nothings in my ear every night.

- Allow me to choose an activity that you will participate in enthusiastically (like a sporting event) once every...

- Go out with the kids for 1-2 hours once every other week so I can have time for myself.

- Tell me that you love me before you leave for work in the morning.

- Surprise me with a small gift "just because" once a month to let me know that you are thinking of me when we are apart.

- Buy a copy of my favorite sports/ hobby/beauty magazine and put it on the coffee table for me to read when I come home.

- Encourage me to take one afternoon, evening, or day per month with my friends.

- Give me a back or foot massage when...

- Take me to my favorite restaurant once every...

Once you are done constructing these lists exchange them with your partner. Keep them in a visible place so that both of you can refer to them regularly. Each of you needs to carry out simple actions once a day. More involved ones can be carried out once a week, month, etc.

I also recommend that couples take time to review these lists once every few months to check your progress and to see how consistent each of you have been. At that time you can add, change, or delete things on your lists. If you are going it alone, give your partner the list to fill out and start working on making things happen for him.

If some things that either one of you included in your list do not make your heart sing after a while, delete it. You probably got used to it and the novelty wore off. Remember to always add something new to replace it. Make sure that your children don't have access to your lists if they contain intimate practices between you and your spouse.

At the risk of being redundant, I would like to re-emphasize at this point that you are primarily responsible for meeting your own emotional needs. Your partner's contribution to your personal happiness is very important, but it should not be the only source of fulfillment for you. This is why it's important to have good relationships with other family members and friends. No single person can help meet all of your needs because that is a tall order for anyone.

If you continue to believe that your partner needs to make you happy, I am sure that you will also keep abdicating to him your responsibility in this area. Please realize that by doing so you are simply giving away the power that you truly possess to generate good things in your own life. Your partner is NOT responsible for your happiness.

I like to say that your partner can be the one who puts the icing on your cake to make it sweeter by making positive contributions to your happiness and wellbeing. You are personally responsible for baking your own cake. It will be rewarding for you to facilitate good things in your personal life. This releases your partner to add to your happiness something extra so that you experience his love.

CHAPTER 8: LET'S TALK

"Give me the gift of a listening heart."   King Solomon

I don't want to stereotype, but in many marriages the wife's simple request of "let's talk" makes the average man want to run away. He anticipates that his wife is going to accuse him of having done something wrong, and he typically tries to avoid such an exchange. And when he does talk with her, he has the tendency to attempt fixing the situation by telling her what she should do. In the process he usually minimizes or dismisses what she is communicating, completely missing what she truly wants or needs from him.

Interestingly, most men are married to women who like to talk, sometimes just for the sake of talking. For the average woman, talking with her husband is the primary way by which she connects emotionally with him.   She wants her husband to listen, not just with his ears, but with his heart. She wants to feel her partner's presence to experience connection with him. She wants to know that he is interested in her.

The majority of married women I have helped express frustration in this regard. They find that their legitimate need for emotional connection through meaningful communication with their partners is not being met. They tell me that when their partners avoid engaging them in conversation they end up feeling as though they have been talking to themselves, and feeling very lonely in the process. It's no wonder that many of these women resort to yelling, nagging, manipulating, or simply shutting down emotionally. Some even get anxious and depressed.

Their husbands don't seem to understand that if they were to have meaningful communication with their wives, they would be helping build safety in their marriage. When partners allow each other to express "the good, the bad, and the ugly" in an honest, yet respectful manner, there can be a genuine meeting of their minds and hearts.

Safety is the bedrock of a healthy marriage because it builds trust, and when there is trust, there can be true intimacy. This is essential in the process of creating a strong marriage, as it allows partners to get close. They discover that the world does not come to an end when they disagree, have a negative experience, differ in their opinion, or even face conflicts that require resolution.

In an atmosphere of safety you and your husband will be able to bring all aspects of your personalities, not just the ones that are deemed to be acceptable. When partners don't feel accepted by their spouse they end up feeling like they are walking on eggshells. This forces them to be disingenuous, fake, or downright dishonest with each other.

If we were to look at men and women from a cultural

and social perspective, we could say that, generally speaking, men are socialized to provide, solve problems, fix things, and protect. Women, on the other hand, are socialized to be nurturers who focus on providing love, care, and facilitating relationships.

These traditional and distinct roles were fully adopted in previous generations, and in many ways defined the main duties, the image, and even the worth of men and women in society. In this day and age, however, things have evolved, and married couples find themselves having to redefine themselves in this regard.

While the cultural framework from prior generations is still present, the majority of couples use it more as a construct that they can use as a point of reference to create their own framework, not as the standard to be followed. Studies show that traditional gender roles have less influence on modern couples who find that, while male and female roles are still important, they need to redefine them in their marriage to make it work.

Instead of having their roles rigidly defined as before, husbands and wives presently define their roles in practical ways that work for them. This is quite possible when spouses create a good blend of their primary roles, with a good degree of flexibility that allows them to work in tandem.

Wives want their spouses to help with household duties

and parenting, for example. Husbands, on the other hand, want their counterparts to go to work outside the home and help earn a living. The bottom line is that both partners are finding that shared responsibility in most aspects of their relationship is helpful to them.

I would say that the most effective way of achieving a satisfactory degree of functionality and cohesiveness in marriage is through effective communication and joint action. This is a vital formula for success. You and your partner cannot expect to have a happy marriage if you fail to communicate well with each other. The two of you will be able to solve problems, make decisions, and come to a consensus about most concerns in your marriage by sharing your ideas, feelings, needs, values, goals, and concerns.

As a couple you also need to communicate with each other about your dreams, wishes, desires, preferences, and expectations regarding all aspects of your marriage. You need to negotiate and reach an agreement when you disagree. You also need to collaboratively take action and implement plans to make your marriage work. Such essential practices need to be maintained and improved over time to keep your marriage alive.

The majority of couples I have coached tell me that they never talked about such important things prior to getting married, or even during the course of their marriage. Others have told me that they talked about them once upon a time, but did not touch these subjects since. You and your spouse may be one of those couples.

If you want a marriage that really works, ongoing and meaningful communication that goes beyond just sharing information must be practiced. Good communication allows partners to connect emotionally by listening, sharing, and by being accountable to each other. In the process they are able to demonstrate that they respect and value each other's perspective, and are able to generate effective solutions to their concerns and problems.

Some couples I have worked with have told me that in the beginning of their relationship they were able to talk and solve problems easily, but with the passage of time somehow they lost this ability. The truth is, the ability was not lost, it was just neglected and forgotten. If this is your case, you and your partner still have it, so it's just a matter of bringing it back.

Even if you and your mate did not develop this ability in the early stages of your relationship, you can do so now. Having said that, it would be helpful at this point for you (and your partner) to take some time to think about the underlying reasons for your communication problems, as they may indicate that there are deeper issues which need to be corrected.

Discovering these reasons will give you important clues as to the dynamics that were established in the marriage from the start. You see, patterns of interaction between lovers get established from the moment they say hello for the first time. Subsequent interactions help cement these in place, resulting in unspoken agreements between them, which will continue to dictate how they will interact once they marry.

For example, Mattie and Pete came to see me when almost all was lost in their marriage. Both complained that there was very little communication between them at that point. They reported that when they tried to communicate, it was in the form of yelling matches that left both of them exhausted and deeply wounded.

This couple described a history that began with Pete dazzling Mattie with his impressive achievements, good looks, and earning power. It was very clear that he had become a highly skilled and successful professional in his field, which gave him an air of superiority and sense of power in the marriage.

Mattie had always wanted to marry someone who was handsome, highly intelligent and accomplished. And of course, it had to be someone who would be able to provide her with a very comfortable lifestyle and grant her a better social status than others in the family.

Interestingly, she was also intelligent and accomplished, but she did not consider her own success to be of the same caliber as Pete's. Being second to the youngest in her family, Mattie learned to admire her brothers, who were clearly favored in the family.

Mattie grew up in a very traditional home where her father was the authority figure who did not bother to communicate with his wife about anything of real importance. He also made all the decisions in the family. Her mother was the nurturer who looked up to her husband, and followed his direction on most things.

Mattie did not recall any experiences as a child where she witnessed her parents interacting meaningfully with each other. Their interactions were limited to dealing with the superficial things of daily life. She did not see her father take a personal interest in her mother or the family, for that matter.

Mattie grew up feeling quite unimportant in her family. When her father died during her adolescence, her mother became depressed, angry and very dominant. She had no patience, simply barking orders at the children. Her mother didn't even notice the emotional pain that the children were experiencing through this entire ordeal. This pretty much summarized Mattie's experience with communication while growing up.

It's no wonder that when she met Pete she felt familiar with him because he was a dominant individual who communicated his superiority in verbal and nonverbal ways. He frequently told her that he was right, and she was wrong. He also interrupted her and raised his voice when she ventured to give an opinion. So she got the familiar message that she was unimportant. Mattie did what she usually did in her relationships with men. She followed the pattern of acquiescing to Pete in every way because, after all, he was so "wise and perfect" for her in so many ways.

Because of these troublesome dynamics the marriage had become one where Pete was more of a parental figure than a husband, and Mattie was more of a child under his authority. Soon she found herself walking on eggshells around him to avoid his temper or putdowns. After a while she realized that she was no more than an extension of Pete.

The day came when Mattie had enough of this and began to fight back. At first she did it with complaints, then with tears, silence, and manipulation. But Pete would not have it. He was determined to keep his position of power and authority, and he made sure to put Mattie in her place every time they had a disagreement. So he added a good dose of criticism to keep her there.

But he also "rewarded" her by buying her expensive things and giving her a lavish lifestyle which she would not be able to afford on her own. He would show her off to his friends and colleagues like a trophy. In public he would treat her like a lady, but at home it was quite a different story.

Of course, Mattie eventually reached a boiling point and resorted to yelling, accusing, and blaming. The line of disrespect moved a little more every time they had a heated argument, both of them spewing greater insults that were very hurtful.

Before quitting the marriage they decided to get professional help. I can only say that this couple had to work hard to learn effective communication skills which helped them to create a marriage that was based on respect, safety, and trust. Had they not done so, I am sure that they would have divorced.

Your marriage may not be in such a terrible state, but you are probably familiar with the typical scenario of not being able to talk with your mate as true partners and soul mates. This is a very common concern that baffles many marriages. You may want to answer the following questions to gain more perspective in this regard.

- Do you feel like you are talking to yourself when you try to talk to your spouse?

- Does he frustrate you by giving you answers or solutions you haven't even asked for, and don't even make sense to you?

- Do you find yourself yearning for emotional connection with him?

- Do your conversations with him get derailed into needless arguments?

- Have you noticed that you are avoiding subjects which would make your husband uncomfortable or upset?

- Do you get exasperated when talking to your husband?

- Are you persistently misunderstood by your mate?

- Do you talk to him about your concerns but nothing gets resolved?

- Do you feel like you and your mate consistently miss what is being said?

An affirmative answer to any of the above questions indicates a problem in communication. Keep reading so you can learn how to improve your ability in this important area.

In my work of teaching good communication skills to couples I have heard many husbands say things like, "I just want to move on. I don't want to talk about the past. My wife is stuck there and just wants to talk about the same problems!" Wives usually say, "I can't talk to him about anything, he doesn't listen. He just tells me what to do and wants me to move on!"

What these folks need to understand is that poor communication creates more marital conflicts which compound the problems that already exist. If the majority of these conflicts are not resolved, they will keep coming up again and again, creating additional distress for both partners, and for their relationship.

Spouses who don't know how to communicate well are usually not listening to each other and resort to deflecting or shouting. Or they simply decide to avoid talking, period. But even that conveys a message, whether they realize it or not.

Good communication is a lot more than just talking. It's a meeting of hearts and minds for the purpose of being intimate with each other. Think of the word intimacy; it really means "into-me-see." All humans want to be seen, listened to, perceived, attended to, understood, and experienced by their partner.

Effective communication is the art of "knowing" your partner and "being known" by him through meaningful interaction. This experience allows spouses to develop what neuroscientists call "emotional attunement", and like musicians in a symphony, mastering the art of being on the same page and creating harmony with their music.

Almost every couple I have helped tell me that they have communication problems. What they are usually referring to is unresolved chronic conflict which has existed between them for a long time. As is typical of this scenario, both partners are struggling for power, and want their needs met. Both are talking, but neither is listening. Or they are engaged in a cold war that leads nowhere. And they think that if they keep doing the same things over and over they will get to a better place.

These partners want to be right, and they push to get what they want. But what they are doing is going around and around in circles trying to prove their point. The more they try to prove the other wrong, the more they get stuck in an endless power struggle where they end up as adversaries. This vicious cycle can bankrupt their marriage.

If you and your spouse argue frequently, especially about the smallest things, realize that those surface problems are not the real problem. There is an undercurrent of hurt, unmet needs and unresolved conflict that keeps re-surfacing and seeking resolution. Unfortunately, this vicious cycle can develop into a perpetual pattern where arguing is the only way in which partners interact or notice each other, as negative attention is better than being completely ignored.

Have you experienced this with your partner? If you have, keep reading so you can begin making positive changes. One of the things you may want to do in those moments is ask yourself the following key questions:

- Do I want to be right, or be close to my partner? You can decide and act accordingly. Joyce Meyer says that "The best way to have the last word is to apologize." I believe that this is true, as long as it is warranted.

If you don't even know why you are apologizing, then something is wrong. Or if you apologize for the same things over and over and nothing ever changes, things are out of order. Worse yet, if you end up apologizing for wrongs committed by your mate, think again, as this is a sign of deeper issues in your marriage.

Dr. Robert Subby, a co-dependency specialist defines it as, "An emotional, and behavioral condition that develops as the result of an individual's prolonged exposure to, and practice of, a set of oppressive rules-rules which prevent the open expression of feeling, as well as the direct discussion of personal and inter-personal problems."

A colleague of mine defines co-dependency as, "The train is about to run you over, and his life flashes in front of your eyes." You might do well to consider whether this is true for you and your marriage. If you discover that there is co-dependency in your relationship with your partner, it would be good to seek professional assistance to work on that. You may also attend a Co-Dependents Anonymous support group (CODA) in your community.

But generally speaking, I would suggest that you can't expect to be close to your husband if you argue with him just to prove your point, get back at him, act superior, or put him down. If you want to be truly close to your partner you will need to have the courage to express yourself respectfully, honestly and directly.

Your communication with him needs to include possible solutions to problems in your marriage instead of limiting yourself to complaining or criticizing. This approach will help him not to go into his "quick fix it" mode.

- The next question you want to ask yourself is, How important is this to me? If it is truly important, take the time to address the issues appropriately. Keep reading until the end of this chapter to know how to do it well.

- Finally, ask yourself, Will I even remember this issue five years from now? If the answer is "No", drop it. It's not important. Move on.

Effective communication with your partner needs to include several ingredients in order for it to be meaningful and cohesive. Take time to reflect on each of the following areas so you can begin to improve your ability to communicate well:

1. **Knowing yourself:** Developing a good degree of self-awareness will allow you to be conscious of how your personal history may be impacting your relational ability. Events from the past can affect your self-esteem, your ability to trust and be close to others, as well as your ability to communicate well with them. Become familiar with your beliefs, thoughts, feelings, and behaviors in this regard.

   For example, you may be have experienced your parents interacting with each other through angry exchanges, shouting matches, giving each other the silent treatment, or ignoring problems while pretending that everything was fine between them.

   You may remember that while you were growing up you were not allowed to express your thoughts or feelings because that was taboo in your family. Or you may recall people in your family "walking on eggshells" when conflicts surfaced in order to maintain a delicate balance in the relationships between family members.

   Experiences like these are probably being re-enacted in your marriage, but you may not be aware that you are repeating those learned dysfunctional behaviors, patterns, and dynamics.

2. **Knowing your partner:** Take time to observe and know your spouse. Notice what he says or fails to say, his body language, and how he reacts. Are you aware of his family history, his relationship with his parents, his emotional wounds, the relationship between his parents, and how this impacted him?

It is important that you understand your partner's experiences from the past, as this will give you a greater and more compassionate awareness of him and his relational style. It will also help you to empathize with him.

3. **Creating alignment:** Open your mind to your partner's personal experience, find common ground, and identify with his point of view. Focus on aspects that are the same or similar for both of you. Discovering what you have in common with your spouse will help you identify with him.

Unquestionably, you and your mate will have differences. Appreciate his perspective despite those differences. Each of you will have your own way of seeing things. Different perspectives can make your relationship interesting.

4. **Creating emotional connection:** Open your heart to perceive your partner's emotional experiences in past relationships, and how those relate to his way of relating to you. Try to walk in his shoes and visit his corner of the world with an open mind and an understanding heart. Have empathy for his feelings and how these influence his ability to relate well to you, to express his feelings, and to solve conflicts with you.

5. **Participating and contributing:** Be fully present in your interactions with your partner. When you communicate with him, make sure you are "all there" so you can convey that you are interested and available. This will require you to put aside your preconceived ideas.

   Speak up when appropriate, resisting the temptation to interrupt him. Make suggestions based on your mutual interest or benefit. Offer solutions and refrain from blame and criticism. Be positive in your approach. Express your desires and preferences, what you want instead of what you don't. Be friendly.

6. **Being mindful:** Be mindful of how you express your thoughts and feelings. Express things in a way that makes it easy for him to listen to you and take in your personal experience. Even

more importantly, be a really good listener, even when he expresses things that may be difficult for you to hear. Resist becoming defensive.

7. **Creating resonance:** Provide feedback to your mate in a respectful, constructive, sensitive, and compassionate manner. Make sure to let your partner know that you understand where he is coming from. Let him know that his experience is important and has meaning for you.

Check with him to make sure that what you heard is what he really said to you. This is extremely important, especially at the beginning of the process of learning good communication skills. Most people do not listen well and need a lot of practice with this. Remember that you are not a mind reader. Let him tell you what he wants and needs to tell you. Be receptive to his efforts of letting you into his mind and heart.

You would do well to let him know that you value his willingness to be vulnerable with you by sharing his thoughts and feelings with you. Hold his confidences as a treasure that needs to be protected. Confidentiality will foster a sense of safety in your marriage.

8. **Allow for differences:** Just because you and your husband are married, it does not mean that

you are joined at the hip like Siamese twins. It is very healthy for you and your partner to be separate and different individuals whose ideas, feelings, preferences, dreams, and desires differ.

Convey to your husband that you understand and respect the differences between you. Discovering and respecting these differences will deepen your connection as you demonstrate acceptance of each other.

In this chapter I want to teach you practical, step-by - step effective ways of communicating with your partner. These will help you in other relationships as well. With practice you will become a good communicator.

Please know that what you are about to learn may seem a bit foreign, laborious, weird, or slow at the beginning. Be persistent. Learning good communication skills is like learning a new language, so you have to start slowly. Experiencing small successes will build your confidence as you go along. This style of communication will, in time, become second nature to you.

The process closely resembles that of learning to dance as a couple. If you have taken dance lessons with your spouse, or have watched "Dancing with the Stars" on television, you have probably noticed that it's difficult at first. Partners may step on each other, fall, and get frustrated. It can be messy, challenging, cumbersome, and discouraging. Some of them even want to quit in the early stages of the competition.

As the couple keeps practicing and putting lots of hard work into refining the skills they are learning together, however, they get much better, even excellent at it. With consistency and commitment they learn to move in unison, making complex routines look easy and beautiful.

Likewise, communicating with your partner can, in time, become a seamless process of synchrony and beauty as you develop your skills. And just like many of the dancers in the show lose excess weight, you and your partner can also lose the weight of the excess baggage you have been carrying around for years. You will feel lighter, stronger, more confident, and HAPPY!

So let's move forward with your process of becoming a good communicator. You may have heard that communication has two main aspects to it: verbal and non-verbal messages. Psychology professor and researcher Albert Mehrabian found in his famous studies that human communication is comprised of 65% non-verbal language (body language), and 35% verbal language.

In order for communication to be good, these two need to be congruent and in balance with each other. Be aware of what you communicate nonverbally with your eyes, tone of voice, volume, posture, facial expressions, intonation, gestures, etc. This next exercise is taken from Imago Therapy, with my own adaptation.

STEP 15 - EXERCISE FOR IMPROVING COMMUNICATION

To learn and practice basic communication skills you will need to go through the following process. Ask your partner to think of something that he would like to talk to you about. Make sure that you and your partner stay on one topic per dialogue. It's OK for you to keep this book in front of you. Tell him that you are practicing a new skill that can help you become a better partner. I am sure this will peak his interest.

You may want to read through this section before you get started. After you do that, ask your partner to tell you what he wants to talk to you about in two short, concise sentences.

1. **Be a good listener:** This is probably the most difficult skill to master because most of us do not learn to listen well. When someone starts talking, we immediately begin to formulate a retort that causes us to stop listening. Suddenly, what we have to say is more important than what the other person has to say. When two people do this, they completely miss each other, or they clash with each other. This is how arguments begin, and how they escalate.

To become a good listener, pretend that you are a radar receiving your husband's transmissions when he speaks to you. Take in his words and observe his nonverbal expressions. Put yourself aside, and don't let your own narrative interfere.

This is called "attentive listening" or "active listening" in the fields of Communication and Psychology. Do not interrupt him or interject your own stuff. He is on the stage, and you are his audience.

2. **Provide reflective feedback:** After listening to your partner you want to let him know that you captured both the words and the essence of his message. This is crucial for good communication because people have mental filters and defense mechanisms which cause them to hear what they want to hear, not what the other person actually expressed.

    In this part of the exercise you want to say back to him what you heard, using as many of the words that he used, without your personal interpretation. Do so in the following manner:

    a) Start by saying: **"What I heard you say is…", or "I understand you to say that…"**

    b) Then ask him if your reflection is accurate: **"Did I hear you well?"**, or **"Did**

I understand you correctly?" If you didn't, he will let you know. Reflect back to him any corrections he makes to fine tune the message until you get it correctly.

c) He can then tell you one or two more sentences on the same topic. You continue reflecting what he shares. To do this, ask, **"Would you like to share more about that?"** He can add two or three additional things to his message, and you reflect what he says.

3. **Provide validation:** When you validate what your spouse expresses to you, you are making sense of what he is saying. You may completely agree with what he has said, agree in part, or disagree altogether.

Validation is not about whether you agree or not. It's about conveying to your partner that what he has said is of value to you. Try to see things from his perspective. To do this you can say something like: **"What you say makes sense because..."**, or **"I could see how you would think that way because..."**

You can do this even if you can only identify with his experience in a general sense. The point is to convey to him that you are trying to see things from his perspective.

4. **Express empathy:** When you empathize with your partner you are walking in his shoes, truly knowing his emotional experience. You are joining him in his corner of the world. This is the level at which couples are able to achieve what neuroscientists call "emotional resonance", or "feeling felt" by the other person. At this level partners connect more deeply and feel emotionally attuned. This allows them to know each other intimately.

> a) You can convey empathy to your husband by imagining how being in his shoes would be like, and telling him, **"I could see how you'd feel..."** **List several feelings you imagine he may be feeling (like sadness, frustration, anger, fear, hope, compassion, guilt, disappointment, hopelessness, excitement, shame, etc.)**

> b) Then you can ask him, **"Is that how you feel, or are there feelings I have not mentioned?"** He may tell you that he feels x, y, or z feelings, or even mention others that you missed. **Empathize with those too.**

5. **Express gratitude:** At the end of the talk you want to thank him for sharing with you. You may also want to tell him the most important or meaningful aspect of what he has shared with you, or what touched your heart in a special way. This is usually the "golden nugget" that both of you will remember the most and take away from the conversation.

PRE-VALIDATION

Dr. Terry Real came up with the brilliant idea that one of the most helpful things that partners can do when they don't understand each other, or when one does something that upsets the other, is to engage by offering pre-validation. This allows them to elicit information, increase their understanding, and engage in helpful communication.

Pre-validation sounds like this: "Darling, I don't really understand where you are coming from, but as soon as you tell me about that, it will begin to make sense to me…" Or, "Honey, I am not sure that my perception of you is right, but I know that if you explain things to me about what just happened, I will be able to see your perspective on it."

This is a very helpful skill that can help prevent a lot of

disruptions and misunderstandings with your mate. Pre-validation is also very helpful because with it partners communicate their basic underlying assumption that the other is coming from a good and sensible place within themselves. It conveys respect and curiosity regarding the logic, truth, reality, or perspective, which guides and makes sense to them.

Try it, this really works. It will prevent defensiveness, facilitate conflict resolution, and achieve satisfactory outcomes for both of you. Additionally, you and your partner will perceive each other as benevolent and fair in your perception of each other.

Drs. Pat Love and Stephen Stosny say that when you only use your own perspective to look at any particular issue you are looking at things through a single lens, and having "monocular vision." This unique perspective is based on your personal experiences from the past, which is the mental filter that your mind uses to perceive and evaluate things.

Stosny and Love say that when partners take in each other's perspective, on the other hand, both of them are able to look at a situation through a set of "binoculars", which helps them to integrate the points of view of both. Only then can they see the whole picture. This practice will allow you to feel connected, respected and important in each other's world.

So I encourage you to find time for friendly conversation

with your partner. If you do, you will notice that the lines of communication begin to open. In time you and your partner will start looking forward to spending more time together and engaging in meaningful conversations. I would suggest that you start with positive topics at the beginning. As you get better at it later on you can take on more challenging ones. This practice will help increase the level of trust and safety between you and your partner.

Here are some topics that can get you going:

- What I love the most in you is...

- My favorite fun activity with you is...

- The time we were together that I remember the most is...

- The things that attracted me to you when we first met were...

- The things that have caused me to love you more are...

- The thing that has surprised me the most about you is...

- What I wish for us the most is...

- One thing that you could do to help me feel accepted by you is...

- What I miss the most in our marriage is...

- What I would be willing to do to bring back the fun in our relationship is...

- One exciting thing I would like for us to talk about is...

- What prevents me from talking to you about my problems or concerns is...

- The thing that makes me most anxious about our marriage is...

- The one thing that makes it most difficult for me to connect with you is...

- I have trouble telling you how I feel because...

- My greatest fear is that...

- One thing I want to change about me is...

- The most positive thing I've noticed in you recently is...

- What is important to me about us is...

- The biggest change I've noticed in me since we married is...

- One thing I am willing to try to improve our relationship is...

- What I am willing to provide for you is...

- What I am ready to do to take care of myself is...

- Your greatest contribution to our marriage and family is...

- I consider my greatest contribution to you and our family to be...

- What I would enjoy doing with you is...

- One thing that would make me feel connected to you is...

- What I wish we had time for is...

- The best aspect of our family is...

- One thing that you and I are great at is...

- My greatest desire for our life as a couple is...

- The thing that you and I share which I value the most is...

- One thing I have learned about you recently is...

- One thing I have learned about me recently is...

- What I need to apologize to you for is...

- One thing I need to ask you to forgive me for is...

- What I respect the most in you is...

- One area where I need your support the most is...

- The problems in our marriage remind me of...

- I have the hardest time when you talk about...

- I really enjoy hearing you talk about...

- The thing that makes me most uncomfortable is...

- One thing I want to learn to do is...

- One thing I want to stop doing is...

- My greatest joy comes from...

- My greatest struggle is...

- One aspect of our marriage that makes me feel secure is...

- One thing I want to celebrate in you is...

- One thing I want to celebrate in me is...

- What I wish for you is...

- One concern I have about us is...

- I believe the key to our happiness is...

- I get very frustrated when...

- I have been distancing from you because...

- You inspire me by...

- What I admire the most about you is...

- The most meaningful thing you have done for me since we met is...

- The most helpful things you do for me are...

- The fondest memory I have of us is...

- My highest aspiration for you is...

CHAPTER 9: FACING THE DRAGON (TOGETHER)

"The harder the conflict, the more glorious the triumph."
Thomas Paine

Let's begin with the realistic premise that conflict is a part of life. Professional Coach Adriana Doyle once said that "the only difference between stumbling blocks and stepping stones is the way in which we use them." Many couples see their conflicts as insurmountable obstacles that block their way or threaten their relationship.

What most couples don't realize is that conflict is an important aspect of marriage, and that it can be their ally instead of a vile dragon they need to run away from. Unfortunately, many couples allow conflicts to destroy them and their relationship. So the decision they have to make is whether they want to face conflict as adversaries, or get on the same team to work together and resolve it.

You and your mate have to make a choice regarding how you view conflict in your marriage, how you approach it, and whether you use it to your collective advantage. You may be thinking that this is easier said than done, and you are right. It won't be easy, especially at the beginning. Yet if you have done the exercises in the previous chapters, it is quite possible that you and your husband will likely be ready to take on this important challenge.

The two of you may soon discover that when conflict is handled properly, it can help you bond at a deeper level and strengthen your partnership in the process.

When couples take an adversarial "You're wrong, I'm right" approach when dealing with conflict, they quickly realize that it just doesn't work. Despite that, many couples keep on doing the same thing over and over, expecting something different to happen. It is no wonder that many of them in time learn to simply avoid conflict at all costs. The proverbial elephant is in their midst, but neither is willing to deal with it by taking a different approach.

Avoiding conflict does not work because it does not solve anything. Unresolved conflicts tend to rear their ugly head somewhere else in the relationship. They also show up again and again, increasing the frequency of relational disruptions and emotional distress between partners.

Do you remember the research by Drs. John and Julie Gottman, which concluded that in order to keep a marital relationship in a healthy place there needs to be a ratio of 5 positive interactions for each negative interaction? Based on that fact we can also conclude that it is simply impossible to maintain this ratio when the negative interactions between spouses predominate by a large margin.

You and your spouse need to remember this because poorly handled conflicts have great potential for ruining a marriage. Frustrated partners gradually distance from each other to avoid additional distress.

This results in a deterioration of the general atmosphere of their relationship, as the emotional connection between them is disrupted. Eventually they start avoiding the conflict and each other as a way of maintaining some degree of homeostasis in their relationship.

Conversely, unresolved conflicts can become a real point of contention which are used as the spark that ignites frequent arguments between partners. These unresolved disagreements usually begin with some innocuous, unimportant, or unrelated issue that culminates in repeated relational disruptions that erode every aspect of the marriage.

If you and your partner have adopted an adversarial approach, chances are you are caught in endless rounds of ineffective conflict resolution. You may be stuck in a pattern where the only way in which the two of you engage or get attention from each other is by starting arguments.

I am quite sure that these have escalated, causing more serious damage to your relationship. This is particularly true if disrespect and character assassination have been allowed. If so, it may be good for you to take some time to answer the following questions:

- Has the frequency and intensity of the fights with your partner increased over time?

- Have you noticed that the arguments seem to start over something small and insignificant?

- Do prior conflicts or resentments resurface in your arguments, and in the end neither one of you remembers why the fight started?

- Do you or your spouse behave inappropriately during those fights?

- Are you and your partner constantly struggling for power?

These are red flags that should tell you that your marriage needs attention, and that you and your husband need to learn a better style of conflict resolution. The developers of Imago Therapy maintain that after the romantic stage of a committed relationship partners enter the "Power Struggle" phase, which is when conflict shows up in Technicolor.

They view this stage in the relationship as a constructive force where conflict can be used to create interpersonal closeness, deeper emotional intimacy, and a meaningful love experience. I fully agree with this concept, as I have repeatedly experienced it in my own marriage, as well as in my work with many couples who have learned to use conflicts as stepping stones rather than stumbling blocks.

I must say that the key to effective conflict management is, without doubt, effective communication. The basic communication exercise in the previous chapter can prove to be very helpful for you. You need to learn and master those skills. They are essential for resolving conflict. You will be able to experience emotional connection with your partner in the process.

If you and your partner learn to communicate in that manner, you will succeed in this crucial aspect of marriage. You may even be able to "agree to disagree agreeably" about unsolvable issues where your positions are diametrically opposed.

Most of the time, however, you will be able to see eye to eye if you engage each other in a way that fulfills your needs, as well as the needs of the situation. The process will also allow both of you to collaboratively generate solutions to your problems.

The following exercise uses the same skills as the previous exercise, but takes your skills to a higher level. With practice you will get better at it, so this is another opportunity for you to practice what you are learning.

STEP 16 - EXERCISE FOR CONFLICT RESOLUTION

I recommend that you attempt this exercise by picking a very small problem or frustration in your relationship with your spouse. This will allow you to take it slowly in order to experience small successes that can encourage you to keep growing in this area. In this manner you and your spouse will be able to build a good foundation that prepares you for greater success in the future as your ability and level of confidence improve.

Resolving small conflicts will also help dissolve some of the negative energy in other levels of conflict in your relationship, and will generate positive energy regarding your ability to solve conflicts collaboratively.

1. Think of a minor issue or problem with your spouse (like his leaving his socks on the floor instead of putting them in the hamper)

2. Take a few minutes to think about this issue from his perspective. Stretch yourself, you will see that you are able to do it.

3. Close your eyes and think about why this is a frustration or problem for you. Is there some unfulfilled desire behind your frustration? Does this remind you of anything in your past? Why is this so important or difficult for you? Could this

be related to some other conflict with your spouse?

4. Take a few minutes to think about potential solutions to this problem.

5. Only after you have gone through this process, ask (do not demand) that your partner grant you 10 to 20 minutes of his time to talk about something that is important to you.

   Make sure and use positive verbal and nonverbal language skills: good eye contact, a friendly smile, good voice tone and volume, displaying an open disposition and body posture, expressing yourself respectfully, etc. If he doesn't have time now, make an appointment to discuss the topic within 24 hours. Set an appointment time that works for both of you, and make sure to show up for your appointment. The process takes no more than 20 minutes.

6. Start the conversation by telling him the topic you want to discuss in **2 short, concise sentences** so he doesn't get overwhelmed.

   Do not allow yourself to go into a long winded discourse. Many husbands tell me that their wives have the habit of saying the same thing in several ways, repeating things over and over. This causes them to feel overwhelmed or stupid.

Keep in mind the prep work you did as you started this exercise. Follow the process outlined below and speak from your own perspective, using short (one sentence) "I" statements:

a) "Thank you for agreeing to talk to me. I wanted to talk to you about..."

b) "This is a concern or problem for me because..."

c) "What is important to me about this is..."

d) "My thinking about this is..."

e) "How I feel about this is..."

f) "What I would like to see happen is..." (Specifically state what you want, need, or prefer in positive terms)

g) "My suggestions on how to resolve this issue are..." (Provide 2 to 3 specific solutions you think are reasonable, doable, and realistic)

h) "What I need from you to help solve this issue is..."

i)   "How that would help me is…"

7. You can continue the conversation if your partner is willing to have a parallel interaction about his perspective on the same issue. If he does, you can continue the process by discussing solutions that could work.

8. Pick one mutually satisfactory solution to experiment with. Agree that if it doesn't work you can always try another solution later on.

9. Determine a reasonable time frame (e.g. one month) to try the chosen solution.

10. Determine specifically how each of you will contribute to solving the problem.

11. Take the corrective action you have agreed upon, and be consistent with it. Many times solutions don't work due to inconsistency.

12. At the end of the experimental period sit down with your spouse to evaluate how well the solution has worked for both of you, and whether your stated goal has been met.

13. If the solution has worked, continue with it. If it has not worked well, attempt another solution and follow the same process until something works reasonably well.

Use the 80/20 rule. If the solution improves the problem about 80% of the time, you are being successful. Get comfortable with this "good enough" principle, and you will be a lot happier for it. Flexibility can make all the difference in many situations.

14. Celebrate your successes. Both of you are worth it. Rewarding yourselves will help solidify your gains in ways that create positive new patterns of thinking, feeling, and behaving in yourself, and in the relationship. This will motivate you and your spouse to solve greater difficulties. It will also build cohesiveness in your marriage.

CHAPTER 10: REWIRING YOUR BRAIN FOR LOVE

"Love looks not with the eyes, but with the mind."
William Shakespeare

Research in the field of Neuroscience has yielded much valuable information about how the human brain works. One of the greatest findings is that of neuroplasticity, which refers to the brain's ability to create new neural pathways and networks through new experiences, changes in behavior, and new mental processes. In other words, you can actually rewire your brain to improve your ability to love, control your emotions, manage stress, and create happiness.

The following exercise is designed to help you do exactly that. Practice it consistently for 10-15 minutes daily (but you can do it for a longer period of time, and as often as you want) You will notice the difference soon enough.

STEP 17 - EXERCISE TO CREATE A LOVING BRAIN

1. Sit on a comfortable chair, preferably in a quiet place.

2. Close your eyes and take some deep breaths as you relax your body, then let your breathing go back to its natural rhythm.

3. Now start noticing the physical sensations that

are associated with your breathing as you follow your breath from beginning to end.

4. Bring to mind a peaceful and enjoyable place where you feel comfortable and relaxed. It could be a place you have visited before, or one that you imagine to be beautiful. It can be a place in your home or in nature (like the beach, a forest, the mountains, a beautiful sunrise or sunset, etc.)

5. As you imagine yourself there, notice the time of day or night, colors, aromas, sounds, and textures that contribute to your sense of wellbeing in this wonderful place.

6. Suggest to yourself that in this haven you feel safe and at peace.

7. Next, feel the healing power of being in this place touching you, going through you, or enveloping you like a comfortable and protective shield.

8. Bring up in your mind's eye the image of your partner and continue to follow your breath from beginning to end. Allow yourself to see him as a human being in need of love and healing.

9. Next, envision some form of loving energy that

emanates from you and goes toward him. It may also radiate from God, reaching both of you. It can take the form of a prayer, a loving intention, or force.

10. Notice how this energy reaches him, touches him, envelops him, or penetrates his being in a transformative or healing way.

11. Then let it return to you and allow it to do the same for you. You may allow this healing force to flow back and forth for a while. Feel the connection with your partner for a minute or so.

12. You may want to take additional time to visualize you and your spouse happily walking down a path where you imagine your life together in one year, five years, and many years down the road.

13. When you finish, re-alert yourself by opening your eyes and taking a moment to notice how your body, mind, and spirit feel in the present time.

14. Finally, make sure that you are fully alert before continuing with your activities.

Note: This exercise is not recommended in cases where your partner has been abusive or destructive to you.

Please see Part 3 of this publication on "Special Circumstances" at the end of the book.

PART 3: SPECIAL CIRCUMSTANCES

I must inform you that there are specific situations where trying to repair your marriage on your own is not indicated, nor recommended. Sometimes marriages can be so damaged or complex that professional help is required to attempt saving the relationship.

Some situations need interventions that go beyond what is presented in this book. The terrain can be delicate or downright dangerous, and I urge you to consult with a psychotherapist. If you find yourself in the midst of one of the situations listed below, it would be prudent for you to get professional assistance. Please refer to the last section of this book and other local resources to find the assistance you need.

1. Physical, emotional, or sexual abuse perpetrated by your partner against you or your children.

2. Substance abuse or addiction to alcohol, drugs, sex, porn, gambling, etc.

3. Chronic or profound mental illness.

4. Infidelity, particularly if it has occurred more than once in the history of the marriage.

HELPFUL RESOURCES

Books:

GETTING THE LOVE YOU WANT

KEEPING THE LOVE YOU FIND

GIVING THE LOVE THAT HEALS

RECEIVING LOVE

GETTING THE SEX YOU WANT

HOW TO IMPROVE YOUR MARRIAGE WITHOUT TALKING ABOUT IT

BOUNDARIES IN MARRIAGE

THE SEVEN PRINCIPLES FOR MAKING MARRIAGE WORK

THE FIVE LOVE LANGUAGES

THE BRAIN IN LOVE

STOP BLAMING, START LOVING

LOVE IS A VERB

THRIVING THROUGH CRISIS

LOVE AND RESPECT

HIS NEEDS, HER NEEDS

REWIRE YOUR BRAIN FOR LOVE

WEBSITES:

www.nellyventurini.com
www.Imago.com
www.aamft.org
www.nicabm.com
www.gottman.com
www.nimh.com

Mental Health Links

The following links are listed to provide you with additional online mental health information and resources.

Addiction and Recovery

Alcoholics Anonymous
Alcoholics Anonymous Recovery Resources
Center for On-Line Addiction
Habit Smart
SAMHSA's Substance Abuse/Addiction
SAMHSA's Treatment and Recovery
Web of Addictions

Anxiety Disorders

Answers to Your Questions About Panic Disorder
National Center for PTSD
Obsessive Compulsive Information Center

Associations & Institutes
American Academy of Child & Adolescent Psychiatry
American Association for Marriage and Family Therapy
American Counseling Association
American Psychiatric Association
American Psychological Association
American Psychological Society
Canadian Mental Health Association
Center for Mental Health Services
National Institute of Mental Health
National Mental Health Association
Substance Abuse and Mental Health Services
Administration

Attention-Deficit Hyperactivity Disorder
ADDA - Attention Deficit Disorder Association
Attention-Deficit Hyperactivity Disorder, NIH
Born to Explore: The Other Side of ADD/ADHD

Child Abuse and Domestic Violence
Childhelp USA®
SAMHSA's Children and Families
SAMHSA's Protection and Advocacy
Questions and Answers about Memories of Childhood
Abuse
The National Domestic Violence Hotline Website

Women, Violence and Trauma
Chronic Fatigue
Chronic Fatigue Syndrome

Depression
Bipolar Disorder News - Pendulum.org
Depression and How Therapy Can Help
Depression NASD
Depression Screening

Developmental Disorders
Asperger's Disorder
Pervasive Developmental Disorders

Eating Disorders
American Dietetic Association
Something Fishy

Journals & Magazines
ADHD Report
Anxiety, Stress and Coping
Autism
Childhood
Dementia
Depression and Anxiety
Drug and Alcohol Review
Dyslexia
Early Child Development and Care
Eating Disorders
Journal of Happiness Studies
Journal of Mental Health and Aging

Journal of Sex & Marital Therapy
Journal of Substance Abuse Treatment
Loss, Grief & Care
Parenting
Personal Relationships
Personality and Individual Differences
Psychology of Men & Masculinity
Psychology Today
Stress and Health
Substance Abuse
Trauma, Violence & Abuse

Medications

Drug Interactions, Alternative, MotherNature
Drug Interactions, DIRECT
Medical Dictionary
Medications, FDA
Medication, Internet Mental Health
Medications, PDR
Medline, Comparison
Multivitamins
SAMHSA's Psychiatry and Psychology

Mental Health General Links

Internet Mental Health
Let's Talk Facts, APA
Mental Health InfoSource
Mental Health Net
Mental Health Resources, About.com
Mental Help Net

Mental Illnesses/Disorders
Online Dictionary of Mental Health
PsychCentral.com
University of Michigan Health Topics A to Z
Web Sites You Can Trust, Medical Library Association

Personality Disorders
Mental Help Net - Personality Disorders
Personality Disorders - Focus Adolescent Services

Suicide Awareness and Hotlines
SAMHSA's Suicide
Suicide Awareness Voices of Education
Suicide, Now is Not Forever
Suicide: Read This First

Additional Resources
Disaster/Trauma
HIV/AIDS
InfoQuit Smoking
Keirsey (Myers-Briggs) Temperament Sorter
NutraSanus.com Natural Health Supplements Guide
Signs of Menopause, Symptoms of Menopause

Note: *Author is not responsible for the content, claims or representations of the listed sites.*

TO CONTACT THE AUTHOR:

(407) 491-8260
www.nellyventurini.com
http://www.linkedin.com/pub/nelly-
venturini/14/9a6/735
nelly.venturini.1@facebook.com
https://twitter.com/nellyventurini

Your reviews on Amazon, Kindle, LinkedIn, Facebook,
Twitter, or any other review form in print or online are
greatly appreciated.

CPSIA information can be obtained
at www.ICGtesting.com
Printed in the USA
LVOW12s1344021117
554749LV00001B/13/P